Evernote

How to use Evernote to Organize & Simplify your Life

Andy Williams, Ph.D.

Version 1.4

What people are saying about this book

"Best *guide* to Evernote." **T. Microft**

"Brilliant guide to using Evernote." **Adam S**

"I consider myself a pretty experienced Evernote user. I have over 2600 notes in Evernote if that's any indication......There's stuff in this book that I was totally unaware even existed as features within Evernote. I just went back to my copy of the book to confirm something for this review and I found something that answers yet another big issue for me related to searching on tags. I wasn't even looking for it and was quite sure Evernote could not do it. Sometimes it's nice to be wrong!" **Stephen Remer**

"This is a gold mine of information on everything you need to know in Evernote. The author seems to be a long time user who writes from the perspective of someone who uses it in the real world. He's done all the tedious work of trying out the various features, then lets you know which ones are truly useful and which are just extra, time-wasting, fluff." **Suzannah Scott-Hughes**

"... if you are using Evernote you really should get this book." **Lloyd**

"I now understand it, thanks to this book by Andy Williams" **Alan Northcott**

"In over 300 well-written pages, he reveals everything you need to know to use Evernote not just as a note-taking tool but as a means of organizing your life. The text is supplemented by copious screen captures, many with helpful annotations." **Mr. N. Daws**

"If you struggle to stay organized online, read this book." **Richard Dennis**

"This book is the most complete guide to Evernote I've ever seen. It is an exhaustive treatment on Evernote and all the features it has... Andy Williams takes the reader from the very beginning, as in how to get started with Evernote on all four platforms that the program can use. The reader is then taught how to customize Evernote, how to archive information, how to share notes, attach files, set reminders and a host of other ways to maximize the value of this program." **New at ereading**

"The more I got involved in online writing services the more I saw the need for being organized. With this guide of "How to use Evernote" I believe this is one of the most comprehensive books that has been written on the subject." **Jim**

Contents

Disclaimer

Before we start, I should just mention that I have no association with Evernote, never worked there, don't know anybody that does or has. This book has been written from my own experiences of using Evernote on different platforms, and is in no way endorsed by Evernote.

That's the simple disclaimer. For those that want a more legally worded one, here it is.

This aim of this book is to get you using Evernote to organize and simplify your life

We'll begin by looking at notes and notebooks. We'll then move on to look at Evernote apps that can be used in conjunction with Evernote before moving onto a comprehensive "How To" section, where I can show you step-by-step details on completing the most common (and some not so common) tasks. Finally, I'll give you some ideas on how you can begin to incorporate Evernote into your life, right now.

Let's take a closer look at Evernote and why you should be using it.

What is Evernote and why should you use it

As the name implies, Evernote is a note taking application, but it does a lot more than just take notes.

For starters, Evernote is a cross-platform tool. That means you can install and use it on PCs, Macs, iPhones, Android devices, all kinds of tablets and your Blackberry, and have near instant access to your notes on any or all of the devices you use.

The cross-platform nature of Evernote is very useful for anyone with multiple digital devices in use every day. Imagine you are out for a stroll with your mobile phone and have a great idea. Open up Evernote on your phone and create a quick note. When you get back to your office, you'll find the note already on your computer, in Evernote, waiting for you to take action.

As you incorporate Evernote into your daily life, you'll find that you can dramatically cut back on the use of paper, and become more organized as a result.

Before I started using Evernote, I had post-it notes all over my computer monitor, scraps of paper covering my desk, and multiple notebooks lined up ready for action. The big problem was that most of these notes just sat gathering dust. It's all well and good scribbling notes and sticking them in prominent places, but trying to find a note several days or weeks later is made all the more difficult by sticky notes losing their stickiness, or gusts of wind blowing paper around the office like confetti. That's not even considering a bigger problem. Often I'd forget that I even made a note about something because with so many pieces of papers floating around, you tend to naturally filter them out.

Now, with Evernote, I can create all kinds of notes (more on this later), and even set a reminder so that I force myself to re-read them and take action at some point in the future. Synced across my phone, tablet, PC and Mac, it doesn't matter where I am, I'll get that reminder. I also have access to all of my notes, wherever I am, since I never go anywhere without my phone.

Now, instead of trying to remember something I'd written on a Post-It note that was stuck on my monitor (like a phone number, or reference number), I can pull out my phone to find the information. Evernote makes finding information easy, with comprehensive search features. You can also make your life a lot easier by organizing your notes in an intelligent manner, something we'll look at later.

Evernote allows you to store all kinds of information, not just typed out notes.

With Evernote, you can:

- Create hand-written notes on touch screen devices,
- Scan and save documents,
- Store photos,
- Create audio notes,
- Attach PDFs or other documents to notes, and
- Set popup and email reminders for any note.

Since Evernote can handle so many different types of content, Evernote users have come up with a wide range of applications for this tool. We'll look later in the book at a few ways in which you can use Evernote to make your life easier, more organized, and less cluttered.

A note about screenshots

Screenshots are an important part of this book. However, Evernote is constantly going through upgrades, and screen appearances can change. In most cases, these are simply cosmetic changes that don't affect the underlying functionality of how things work. If your screen does not look exactly like the one in this book, don't panic. Simply look at your screen and work out where things have moved to.

Versions of Evernote

There are three versions of Evernote, and the version you have will dictate what features you can use.

Evernote Free

The basic free version is fine for most users. The features/limitations include:

- Upload 60MB of data to your account every month,
- Maximum note size of 25MB
- Notebooks are online only,
- Handwriting recognition,
- Share notes with others (who can view them but not edit),
- Attach files to notes.

Evernote Premium

The Premium version currently costs $5 per month or $45 per year. This version adds some noticeable improvements for power users, including:

- 1GB of uploads per month, and the ability to upload larger files (up to 100MB) than the free version,
- Ability to access notebooks offline,
- Note history,
- Faster image recognition,
- Ad-free if you want,
- Add a pin-lock on mobile devices to stop others from viewing your notes,
- Share notes with others (who can view and/or edit),
- Search text in Office docs, PDFs and other attachments.
- Presentation mode.

Evernote Business

Evernote Business is designed with teams in mind and costs $10 per month, per user. It has the same feature set as the Premium version.

With it, you can:

- Share business notebooks with colleagues, the notebooks appearing in their account,
- Presentation mode to share ideas with your colleagues,

- All notes, files, images etc are made available on all of your devices, even offline,
- Related notes help you find relevant notes from your team,
- Keep personal content private.

IMPORTANT if you use Mobile versions of Evernote

Evernote Sidebar on Mobile Devices

Before we begin looking at Evernote, I need to show you how to access the left sidebar on mobile devices (Android and iOS phones and tablets), since this is something I'll ask you to do A LOT in this book.

The sidebar is pretty important as it gives you access to the guts of Evernote. On desktop versions of Evernote, the sidebar is always visible (unless you specifically configure it to be hidden), but on mobile devices, screen real estate is precious, so the sidebar is hidden until requested.

Rather than repeat the instructions every time I need you to open the sidebar, I've put the instructions here.

The mobile devices we cover in this book are Android and iOS (iPad and iPhone), so let's start with Android.

Opening the Sidebar on Android Devices

When you open Evernote for the first time, you'll see this in the top left of the screen:

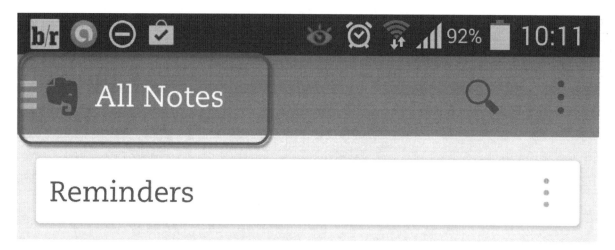

To access the sidebar, tap the elephant's head, or the three horizontal lines to the left of the head.

The sidebar will slide out:

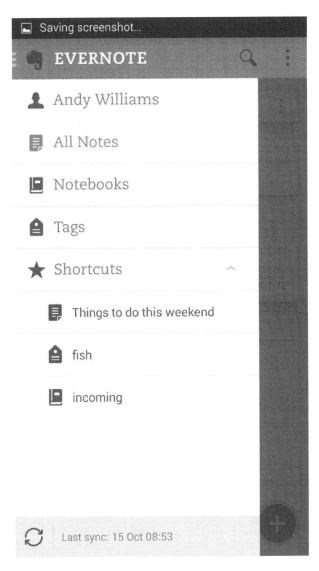

From the sidebar, you can access notes, notebooks, tags, shortcuts, etc.

Any time you want to access the sidebar, tap on the Elephant's head top left, and the sidebar will slide out.

While we are looking at Android, there is a nice setting that I recommend you enable.

To access the settings (which is something else I'll ask you to do in this book), tap on the menu button top right. It's three vertical dots.

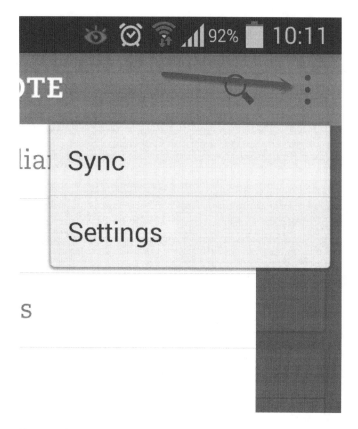

From the menu, tap on **Settings**. This opens a scrollable screen with a lot of different options:

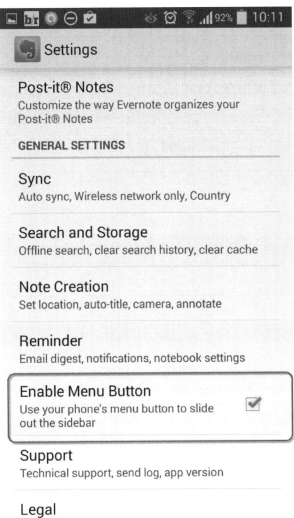

Scroll down until you get to **Enable Menu Button**, and check that option. Now, whenever you press the menu button on your device, the sidebar will slide out. Using the device's menu button is far more natural in my opinion.

Android Evernote Widget
While we are covering Android specific quirks, I should mention the excellent Evernote widget that installs on your Android device. The widget is simple, but gives you quick access to the commonly used features.

Tapping the elephant's head opens Evernote.

The next five buttons are configurable, but the default settings are:

- standard text note
- camera shot
- audio note
- hand-written note.

The final button opens the widget settings. This not only allows you to change the color scheme used by the widget, but also customize those 5 buttons. You can set any of those buttons to carry out any of these tasks:

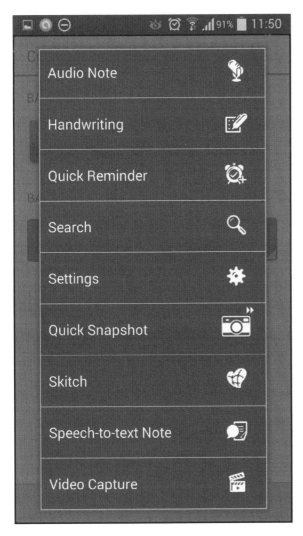

There are a couple more widgets available on Android, like this one:

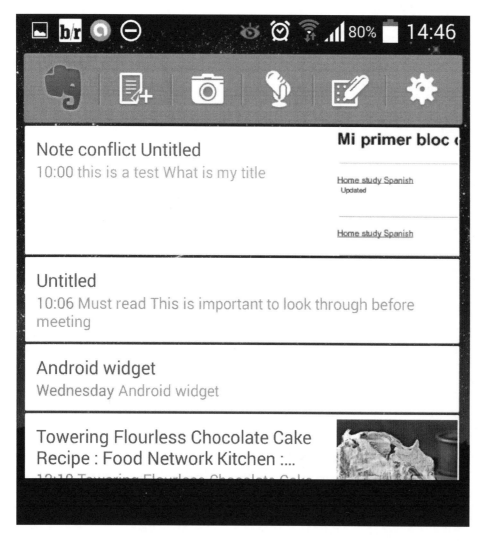

Here you have the buttons as well as some recent notes displayed.

OK, let's look at the sidebar on iOS devices.

Opening the Sidebar on an iPad

When you open Evernote on your iPad, you'll see an elephant's head in the top left of the screen:

Tap the elephant to open the sidebar:

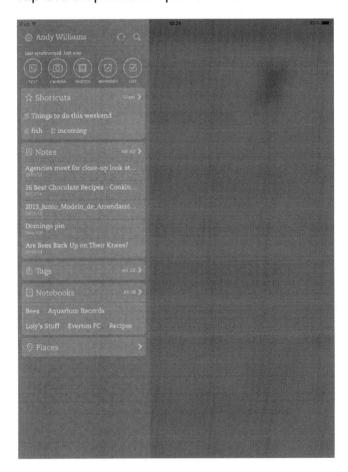

The sidebar slides in from the left and looks similar to the one above. At the very top of this sidebar, you'll see your name and a small "cog" to the left of your name.

Tapping this area of the screen opens up the settings for Evernote. We'll look at that later in the book.

Underneath your name, you can see quick buttons to create different types of notes:

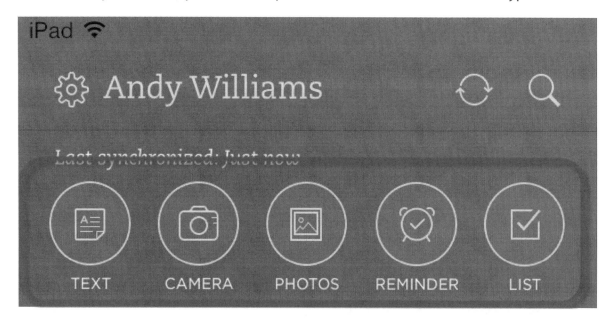

Under these buttons you can access notes, notebooks, tags, shortcuts, etc.

Now, sometimes when you open the sidebar (by tapping the elephant's head) you'll see a different screen. That's because the iOS sidebar is dynamic, and displays the last thing you requested. Let's see an example.

If you tap on **Notebooks** in the sidebar, you'll see the sidebar changes to give you notebook-specific options:

If you close the sidebar, and then re-open it, this Notebook sidebar will be the one you are shown. To get back to the main sidebar we saw earlier, tap on the **Back** button top left.

As you use Evernote, you'll get used to this. If you find yourself on the Notebooks, notes, tags or other sidebar screen, tap the **Back** button to return to the main sidebar.

Opening the Sidebar on an iPhone

The process on an iPhone is slightly different to the iPad version of Evernote, since the elephant's head is missing on the iPhone. However, it is very intuitive.

From any screen other than the sidebar, look for the back link top left. Tapping this will take you back to the previous screen. If that screen is not the sidebar, continue tapping the back button and you will eventually get there.

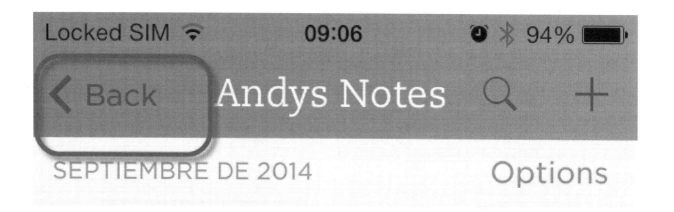

The sidebar on the iPhone actually takes up a full screen:

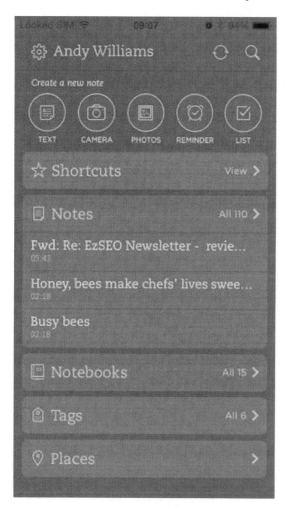

Just like on the iPad, there are easy buttons to create new notes on the sidebar. We'll look at those later.

OK, with the sidebar on mobile devices covered, let's look at Evernote.

Notes

What are Notes?

Notes are at the heart of the way Evernote works. Everything you enter into Evernote is stored in a note or attached to a note.

Think of a note as a single entry in Evernote.

When you add a note, depending on what platform you are using, you can choose to add notes as text, ink (hand-written), images (e.g. camera shot), or audio. You can also attach documents to a note, and even set a reminder date and time for any note.

For example, when your kids give you their latest art masterpiece, take a photo of it and store it as a note. You can even get your kids to record a short audio message and attach that to the note. In the future, when you're old and grey, you can enjoy their art and messages by searching for their artwork.

Every note you add to Evernote has a number of properties, some are added automatically, and others can be added manually if required. These properties include the date the note was created (giving you easy chronological access to those art masterpieces), and even the location if your device has GPS. We'll look at using GPS later in the book. Other properties include the "notebook" that it belongs to, and tags you have assigned to the note (we'll look at tags soon), and a URL, if you want to reference a web page.

I should also mention here that Premium Evernote users have access to note history. Every now and again, Evernote checks to see if a note has changed. If it has, Evernote saves a copy of the old version as well as the new one. That way you can always go back in to see older versions of each note.

Notebooks

You can think of a Notebook in the same way you would a physical notebook. It's a container that holds notes.

In the real world you might use one notebook to record your fishing trips, and another for your favorite cake recipes. Notebooks in Evernote can be used in the same way. You'd have one for fishing trips, where you could add photos of the whoppers you catch, and audio files bemoaning the one that got away. You could even scribble notes on which baits worked best for those particular conditions, and the GPS feature on your phone would record the location of the note; so you could find your way back to that spot in the future.

For your favorite cake notebook you could include the recipes and shopping lists, as well as a photo of the cake.

As you can see, notebooks in Evernote are more dimensional than pen & paper notebooks. They offer you more ways to capture the moment, and better ways of retrieving those moments in the future (we'll look at searching later).

In Evernote you can have up to 250 notebooks.

Default notebooks

In Evernote, you assign one notebook to be your default notebook. When you create a new note, it will be created in the default notebook, unless you specify otherwise.

I personally use a default notebook called "Incoming" which I can then send everything to. I can then move notes to more appropriate notebooks when I have more time.

Local v Synchronized notebooks

You can choose to make notebooks either local or synchronized.

A local notebook is ONLY stored on the device you create it on, and not synchronized with Evernote servers (and therefore not available on your other devices). Synchronized notebooks are uploaded to Evernote and propagate to all of your other devices.

You might decide that some information is best kept only on your device (eg. financial information, PIN numbers, etc), so local notebooks might be useful. However, the real benefit of Evernote is the synchronization of notes. This ensures you have your notes available to you wherever you might be, on whichever digital device you happen to be carrying.

At the time of writing, there is no way of changing a local notebook to a synchronized notebook, or vice versa, so make your choice wisely when you create the notebook. If you do end up needing to switch, there is a work-around involving copying the notes to a new notebook. I'll show you that later in the book.

Notebook Stacks

Just as a notebook is a collection of notes, a notebook stack is a collection of notebooks. Notebook stacks give you yet another way of organizing your notes. Notebooks that are related to one another can be added to the same stack.

A simple example would be a user with two stacks – "Home" and "Work".

The "Home" stack might contain notebooks like:

- Beer reviews
- BBQ recipes
- Liverpool FC
- Kids

The "Work" stack might contain notebooks like:

- Colleagues
- Meetings
- XYZ Project
- ABC Project

And so on...

If you were looking for a particular BBQ recipe to share with a friend, you'd immediately know that the relevant notebook was in the Home stack. Of course, with Evernote's comprehensive search features, you might just simply search for the recipe. However, stacks are a great way of cleaning up the Evernote interface, keeping notebooks logically organized into groups, or should I say **stacks**.

Tags

Tags are yet another way of organizing notes. I'll warn you now - your use of tags will probably evolve over time as you use Evernote. A lot of Evernote beginners either don't use them, or they use so many that tags quickly become useless.

To be honest, the search features in Evernote are so good you may not use many tags, if any at all.

If you are going to use them, my advice is simple. Less is more.

So what is a tag anyway?

Tags are simply words you can use to "describe" your note's content.

The best use of tags is to use them sparingly, and only for those notes you think you might want to pull out later as a group. Ultimately though, your use of tags will depend on how you set up your notebooks.

For example, I might tag all of my recipes that use chocolate with the tag **chocolate**. Then, whenever I want to find a chocolate recipe, I can simply search for the tag **chocolate** and get a list of all relevant recipes.

Alternatively, I might have a notebook stack called recipes, containing several recipe notebooks, e.g. cake recipe notebook, biscuit notebook, Italian notebook, chocolate notebook, and so on.

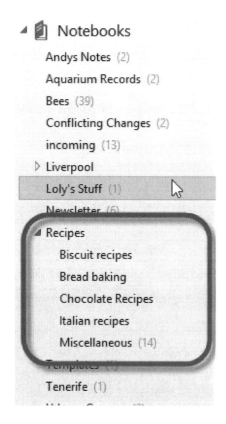

With a notebook devoted to chocolate recipes, there really isn't any use for a chocolate tag, is there?

However, the chocolate tag would be useful if I had a stack called recipes with notebooks like:

- Cakes
- Biscuit
- Puddings
- Ice cream

I could have chocolate recipes in all four of those notebooks, so the best way of pulling out chocolate recipes from all four notebooks would be to tag them with the word **chocolate**.

Let's look at another example of useful tagging, using two main stacks – Home & Work

You might have a notebook called "Kids" in the "home" stack, which contains notes about your two kids, Peter and Jane.

When Peter brings home his school report, take a photograph of it and save it as a note. Tag the note with **Peter**. Whenever Peter gives you artwork, take a photo of the masterpiece and tag it with **Peter**. The same goes for Jane. You'll then have an easy and convenient way to find all notes related to Peter, or Jane, or chocolate recipes for that matter.

To complicate the matter of tags even further, tags can be nested.

For example, you can have a tag for Peter and then created nested tags under Peter for **Artwork**, **School**, **Medical**, **Sports**, etc.

You might think that this would give you further options for displaying your notes, because with a hierarchical system, it's logical to assume that you could display all notes related to **Peter** by simply searching for the tag **Peter**, or be more selective and choose **School**, just to show those notes about Peter related to school. However, there is a slight problem here. Nested tags don't actually function in a hierarchical way, and are really only there for "visual" effect in Evernote's user interface. Having **Artwork** nested under **Peter** does not, in any way, link the **Peter** and **Artwork** tags.

Therefore you cannot then have the same **Artwork**, **School**, **Medical**, **Sports** tags under **Jane**. You can only use a tag once, so if you use **School** as a child tag for **Peter**, you cannot also use it as a child tag for **Jane**. However, because **Peter** and **School** are not actually related, you could tag Jane's notes with **School**, even though **School** is shown in Evernote as a child tag of **Peter**.

In other words, nested tags are really only there to help you clear up an otherwise cluttered list of tags, organizing them so they are visually easier to find.

If this is all sounding too complicated, don't panic. My advice is to leave tags alone for now, and start incorporating them into your notes as and when you feel you need them.

I'd also recommend you forget all about nested tags. Unless your list of tag is really huge, nesting them is probably not something that will help you.

Apps that integrate with Evernote

There are a lot of apps that can integrate (send information to, or edit notes already created) into Evernote, but not all of them are available for all platforms. There are so many that it is not possible to cover them all here, however, I do want to briefly mention the most popular ones.

A great place to look for apps that integrate is here:

http://appcenter.evernote.com/

From that page, click through to your Evernote platform (Windows, Mac, Android, iOS, etc) to see a list of apps compatible with that platform.

The apps are also organized into "Collections", so you can browse through, let's say, the "photography" collection, to find apps related to that topic.

Let's take a look at one of my favorite apps, which works on Evernote for PC.

Foxit Reader (PC)

Foxit Reader is a PDF reader I use on my Windows laptop. I much prefer it to Adobe Reader which I find slower and cumbersome to use.

I read a lot of PDF files for my work, and often it is useful to save the PDF to an Evernote notebook.

Foxit Reader makes this a quick process. You simply open the PDF in Foxit Reader, and go to the Share tab and click the Evernote button:

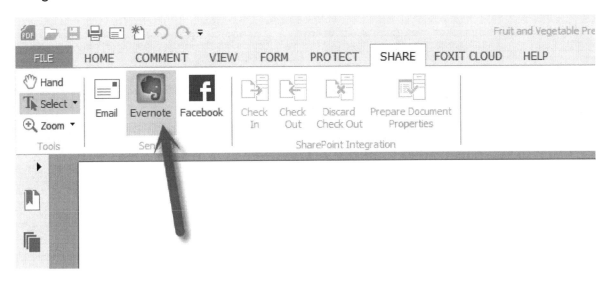

You'll find a growing number of PC, Mac, Android and iOS applications adding in this type of integration with Evernote.

Evernote Web Clipper (Web Browser Extension)

This one is created by Evernote so that you can quickly and easily clip articles, images, or the odd paragraph from a web page, directly into Evernote. It's a web browser extension, and there are versions available for Chrome, Firefox, Safari, Opera and Internet Explorer.

How you use the Web Clipper will depend on the browser you are using. I have it installed in Google Chrome, which is my default web browser, and Web Clipper adds a button to the toolbar, top right:

Clicking this button opens up the option screen:

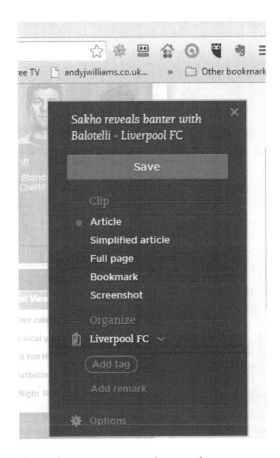

From here we can choose how we want to capture the web page.

Do we want to save the full article, or a simplified version? Do we just want to save the URL as a bookmark, or maybe take a screenshot from the page. If you select screenshot, you'll get cross hairs on the webpage to mark out the region you want to capture.

Another option you have for capturing, is to select a paragraph of text that you want to capture, then click the Evernote button. This will give you the **Selection** option:

You'll also notice the **Organize** section lower down this screenshot. This allows you to change the notebook, or add tags/remarks to the note as it's saved. At the very bottom you can access the Web Clipper options, which control the default actions of the clipper.

Camscanner

CamScanner allows you to digitize receipts, notes, and documents with your phone, and then save them to Evernote.

CamScanner optimizes the image quality so that diagrams and text are sharp. The paid version offers OCR, enabling your text scans to be turned into editable text.

There are also editing tools, allowing you to markup your documents.

Here is CamScanner in action on my Android phone.

Step 1 - start CamScanner, and click the camera button to take a photo of your document.

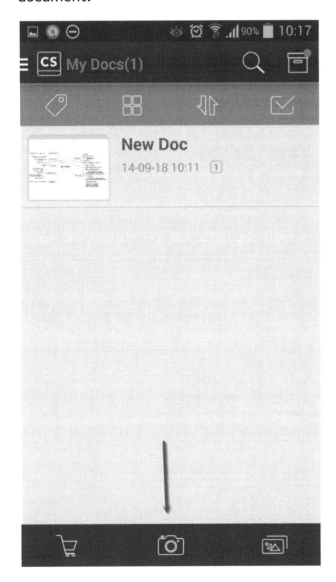

Step 2 – line up the document in your screen:

.. and press the camera button at the bottom to take the photograph.

Step 3 – If necessary, use the draggable bounding box to mark out exactly what part of the image you want to save.

Once the bounding box is enclosing the area you want to capture, tap on the check mark (bottom right) to save.

CamScanner will digitize the image:

You'll notice a few editing options across the top. I'll leave you to play with those.

Once you are happy with it, click the Save button (the check mark bottom right).

The mains screen in CamScanner opens, with your image saved.

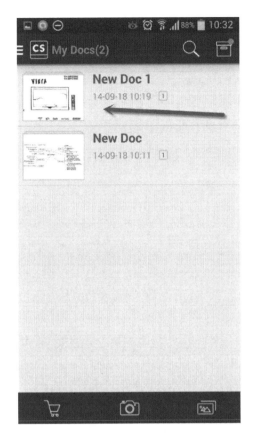

Tap on the image you want to upload to Evernote. This opens the document it in CamScanner:

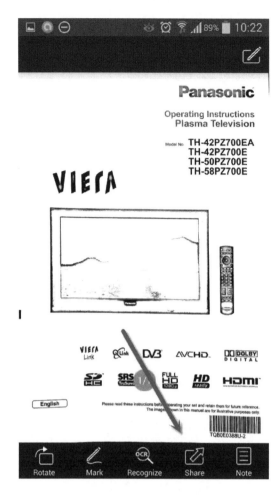

Now click the Share button.

Select Evernote (or anywhere else you want to share the document) and add a note about the image. On sending, the document will be sent to Evernote. Here it is in my Incoming notebook.

Created	Updated	Title	Notebook	Tags	Sync	Size
11/09/2014 08:51	11/09/2014 08:51	Things to do this weekend	incoming	Todo		317B
1 minute ago	1 minute ago	New Doc 1	incoming			346KB
15/08/2014 20:33	15/08/2014 20:34		incoming			142KB
15/08/2014 20:33	15/08/2014 20:33		incoming			166KB
14/08/2014 12:29	14/08/2014 12:29		incoming			623KB

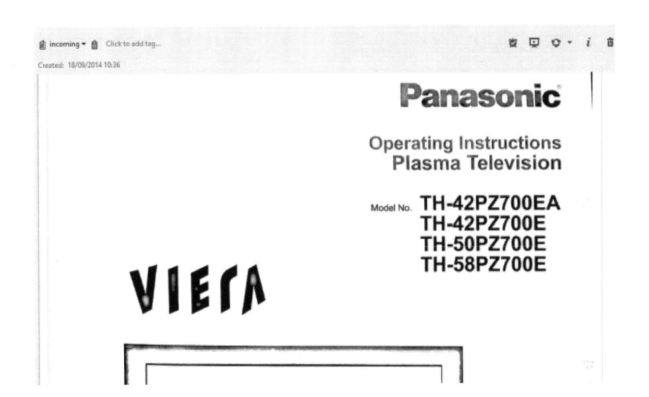

Panasonic

Operating Instructions
Plasma Television

Model No. **TH-42PZ700EA**
TH-42PZ700E
TH-50PZ700E
TH-58PZ700E

VIErA

Skitch

Skitch is a simple drawing program that allows you to create an image, or annotate an existing one, add shapes, annotations, etc.

Skitch is available on iOS, PC, Mac, Android, etc.

On my Android phone, I've loaded the image of the TV manual I took with CamScanner, and added a couple of shapes to pinpoint the model of the TV:

You can see the editing tools along the bottom, and up the right side. These tools popup by tapping the button in the bottom right of the screen.

On the bottom left of the screen is another button that pops up color and brush size tools.

When you are happy with your image, click the Share button.

You'll get a popup asking where you want to share it.

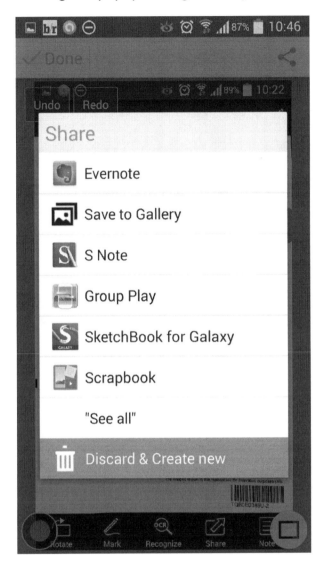

Skitch can be a great way to communicate ideas without having to write lengthy text. What's that saying about images telling a thousand words?

Evernote Clearly

Clearly is a browser plugin that can take a complicated web page, clean it up, and post a nice, easy to read version to Evernote.

Once installed, your browser will have a Clearly icon that you can click to save a simplified, nicely formatted version of a web page to Evernote.

For example, on this Minty Mango Smoothie recipe page, there's a lot going on:

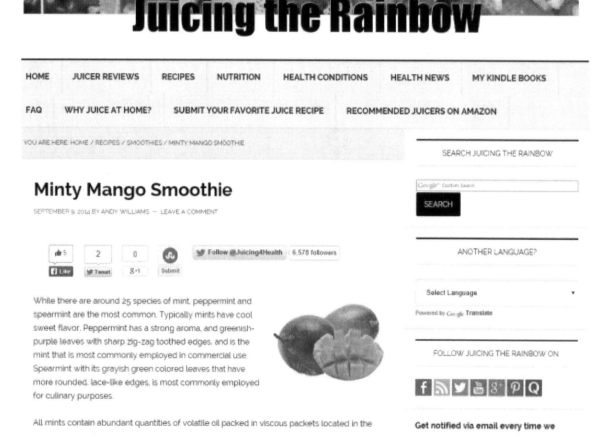

It would be nice if I could just get the recipe.

Well, top right of my Chrome browser is the Clearly button:

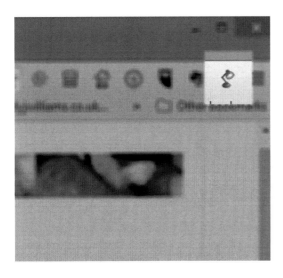

Clicking that gives me an overlay screen with just the recipe information:

You'll notice the Evernote share button in the Clearly toolbar. How cool is that?

Tap it to save the recipe as a note.

Penultimate for iPad

Penultimate is a hand-writing & drawing application that can sync with Evernote. Write, draw, do whatever you want in Penultimate, and then save to Evernote.

Penultimate allows you to change the pen width and color, and can connect to a Jot Script Stylus. You can also use lined paper, graph paper or plain paper, helping you with whatever type of document you are creating. You can also add photos into your notes.

Once you are done, simply share your document with Evernote.

If you are the type of person that likes to write down notes, or draw sketches while you are out an about, forget the paper and take your iPad and Penultimate with you.

You can read more about Penultimate at https://evernote.com/penultimate/

Evernote Hello

Available for iPhone and Android, this application is supposed to make remembering people that you meet a little easier. When you meet someone, you can manually enter them into Evernote Hello, or give them your phone and get them to type in their details.

You can add a photo and notes about the person, and it will even record where you met them.

I suppose if you are out on business a lot, meeting people, this might be a useful application, but it's not one that I use.

More details at https://evernote.com/hello/

Evernote Food

Available for iOS and Android, this application allows you to capture food. Whether it's a great new restaurant you've found, or top secret family recipes, Evernote food allows you to collect everything in one place.

There are a few sections within this app. The two that I find most useful are for my own recipes, and the section on restaurants.

The recipe section is great if you want to take your recipes with you, maybe to share with friends, or to act as a shopping list. Recipes can include a photo of the final product.

Evernote Food allows you to explore recipes online, and save any you like to your recipe book.

The restaurant section of this app uses your GPS coordinates to suggest some places close to your current location, together with scores out of 10 if available (powered by FourSquare). You can of course save your favorite restaurants, or maybe just those restaurants you want to try at a later date.

Everything can be synced and shared with Evernote.

More details at https://evernote.com/food/

Web Apps that Integrate

Web Apps are applications that run in your web browser, and a lot of them integrate with Evernote. Rather than talk you through some of these, I'll let you explore them on your own. This web page has a comprehensive list:

http://appcenter.evernote.com/platform/web-apps

IFTTT

A special Web App mention must go to IFTTT, which stands for If This Then That.

IFTTT is like a robot that you can use to carry out certain tasks whenever pre-defined criteria are met.

For example, suppose you post pictures to Instagram. You might like those pictures to be automatically saved to your Evernote account as well. You could of course send a picture to Evernote immediately after sending it to Instagram, but what if you use multiple devices, some without Evernote already installed. What if you are just too lazy to send the picture to two locations?

Well, you could set up an IFTTT "recipe" to monitor your Instagram account, and any time a new image is uploaded, IFTTT automatically uploads it to your Evernote account.

IFTTT is all about automating tasks.

Perhaps a better example would be for IFTTT to monitor eBay searches. Any time there was a new match in the search results (for an item you want), IFTTT would post that information to your Evernote account.

IFTTT allows you to create your own recipes with almost limitless permutations.

There are also a lot of recipes that IFTTT users have shared with the world, and you can use those pre-made recipes yourself. You can find them here:

https://ifttt.com/evernote

Examples of what you will find include recipes which:

1. Save starred Gmails to Evernote.
2. Make an Evernote journal based on your calendar.
3. Save Craigslist posts to Evernote.
4. Save favorite tweets to Evernote.

5. Allow you to tag a Vimeo video to watch later, and have a note sent to Evernote.
6. Monitor Facebook and backup your photo uploads to Evernote.

As you can see, IFTTT is really very powerful.

Setting up an IFTTT recipe from scratch

Let's set up an IFTTT recipe, so you can see how easy it is to get started.

I like to keep up to date on a variety of topics that I am interested in. One way of doing that is by keeping an eye on Google News for new reports or articles.

Wouldn't it be nice if IFTTT could monitor Google News for me, and send me any new reports directly to Evernote?

Well it can! Let's create the recipe.

You can access Google News at: http://news.google.com

On Google News, I've logged in with my Gmail address and searched for "bee colony collapse", a topic I want to keep up to date on.

If I scroll to the bottom of the page, there is a button to **Create alert**.

Why almonds are bad news for the environment ✓
Quartz - Aug 29, 2014
The industry requires 1.4 million **bee** colonies, according to the USDA, ... Because of **colony collapse** disorder, honeybees are a commodity.

Beware of the Robobee, Monsanto and DARPA ✓
The Indypendent - Aug 20, 2014
Let's consider for a moment the honey **bee** and its anticipated ...
nothing to do with **colony collapse**, and we're sorry that the honey **bee** is dying.

Stay up to date on results for *bee colony collapse*.   Create alert

Google ›
1 2   Next

Clicking it takes me to the alert screen:

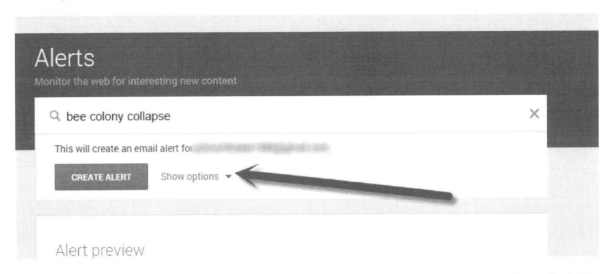

I want to create an RSS feed out of the news search results, so I need to click **Show Options**.

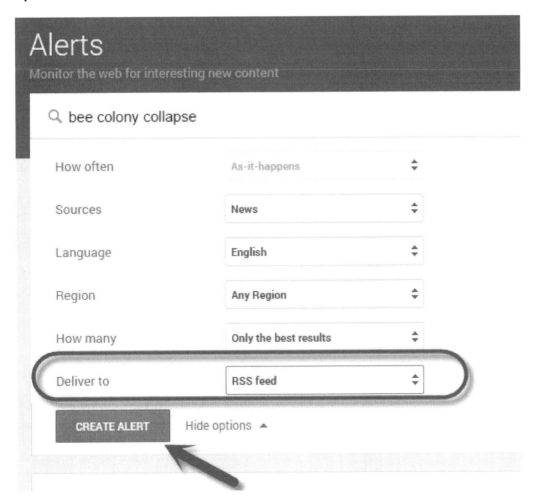

Make sure **RSS feed** is selected in the **Deliver to** field (alternatively you can have the results emailed to you), and click on the Create Alert button. A screen will load showing you a list of all alerts you've set up.

Next to the one we just created is the RSS symbol:

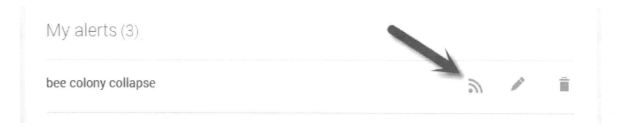

If I click it, Google takes me to the web page for that feed, and I can copy the URL (web address) of that feed from the browser address bar.

OK, with feed URL copied, login (create an account if you don't already have one) to IFTTT and click the **Create a Recipe** button.

Create a Recipe

ifthisthenthat

You'll be taken to the screen above.

What we want to set up is a recipe that can be summarized as follows:

If the RSS feed has a new report, then send it to Evernote.

Click on **this** which is underlined.

In our recipe, **this** refers to finding a new report listed in the RSS feed, therefore, we need to find the RSS feed icon.

Click it.

IFTTT will then ask us to be a little bit more specific about the RSS feed "trigger":

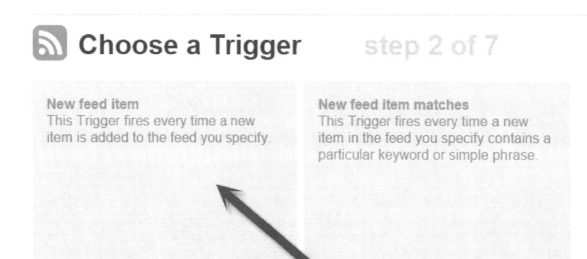

New feed item
This Trigger fires every time a new item is added to the feed you specify.

New feed item matches
This Trigger fires every time a new item in the feed you specify contains a particular keyword or simple phrase.

I want the recipe to be triggered if there is a new report in the feed, so I selected the first item.

IFTTT then asks me for the feed URL, which I copied to the clipboard earlier.

After pasting the URL into the **Feed URL** box:

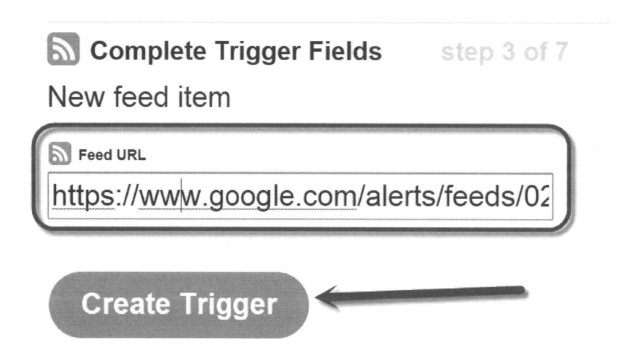

New feed item

Feed URL

https://www.google.com/alerts/feeds/02

Create Trigger

Click on the **Create Trigger** button to move to the next step (where we define what happens when a new feed item is found).

New feed item from
https://www.google.com/alerts/fe
eds/02842712894499255423/10
604688470405973209

So, *if* there is a new report in the RSS feed, **then** we want something to happen.

We define what the something is, by clicking the **that** link.

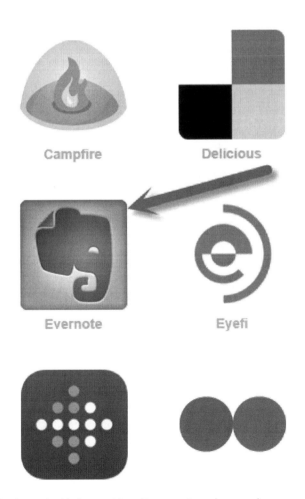

Find and click on the Evernote channel.

The first time you do this with Evernote, you'll be asked to activate the channel.

Click on the Activate button and enter your Evernote login details (IFTTT needs these to create a note) to authorize IFTTT to post.

After authorization is successful, you can click the **Continue to the next step** button.

You will now be given options. What exactly do you want to do when new items are found in the feed (search results)?

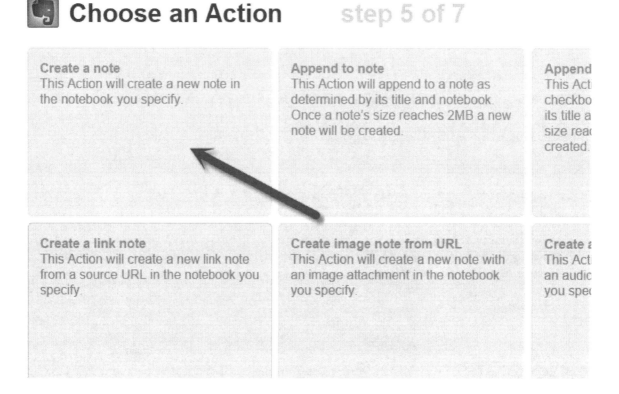

I want to create a note, so that is what I need to click.

You'll now have a screen called **Complete Action Fields**. I am going to leave everything at their default values, except for Notebook, which I am going to change to Bees – the notebook in Evernote I want the posts to be sent to.

Create a note

This Action will create a new note in the notebook you specify.

Title

EntryTitle

Body

EntryContent

via FeedTitle EntryUrl

Notebook

Bees

Leave blank for default notebook

Tags

IFTTT, FeedTitle

Comma separated

Click the **Create Action** button to complete this step.

On the next screen, enter a short title and click the **Create Recipe** button. The recipe will be saved and activated automatically, but it might be a few hours before you notice anything turning up in your Evernote notebook.

Here is a screenshot from my Evernote account 24 hours later:

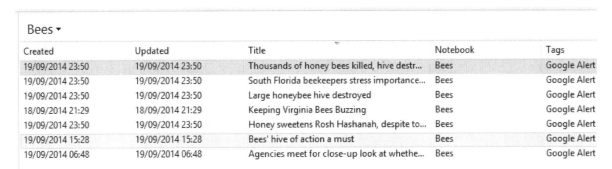

Bees ▾				
Created	Updated	Title	Notebook	Tags
19/09/2014 23:50	19/09/2014 23:50	Thousands of honey bees killed, hive destr...	Bees	Google Alert
19/09/2014 23:50	19/09/2014 23:50	South Florida beekeepers stress importance...	Bees	Google Alert
19/09/2014 23:50	19/09/2014 23:50	Large honeybee hive destroyed	Bees	Google Alert
18/09/2014 21:29	18/09/2014 21:29	Keeping Virginia Bees Buzzing	Bees	Google Alert
19/09/2014 23:50	19/09/2014 23:50	Honey sweetens Rosh Hashanah, despite to...	Bees	Google Alert
19/09/2014 15:28	19/09/2014 15:28	Bees' hive of action a must	Bees	Google Alert
19/09/2014 06:48	19/09/2014 06:48	Agencies meet for close-up look at whethe...	Bees	Google Alert

There were 7 new notes linking to articles of interest, and I get to see these on all of my devices running Evernote. Even better, I no longer need to keep an eye on Google News.

If there is a particular website you want to keep up to date with, you can look for an RSS feed on that site and create a similar recipe to the one shown above. Whenever new content is posted on that site, the RSS feed adds the article at the top of the feed, and IFTTT will spot it and post the information to your Evernote notebook.

That was quite easy, wasn't it?

Sign up at http://ifttt.com to get started and see how your life can be automated.

How to use Evernote – Hands on!

You can do most things in a variety of ways. The first way is to login to the Evernote Web application (login via Evernote.com).

Where applicable, I'll show you how to do things through the Evernote Web first, then the same procedure in Evernote applications on a PC, Mac, Android device and iOS device.

I should point out that at the time of writing this book, Evernote are trialing a beta version of Evernote Web. The new version looks nice, but has most of the functionality stripped out. I guess the idea behind this is to let web users concentrate on the most important things – notes and notebooks, while removing everything that can cause distraction, and are probably best saved for Desktop and mobile versions of the application.

In this book, I've used the normal, stable version of Evernote Web, ignoring the beta version. I am really hoping that when the beta is fully released, Evernote allows its users to choose between the new simplified interface, and the older established one. If the beta is forced on everyone, I'll update this book accordingly.

Evernote Accounts

Setting up an Evernote account

To set up an Evernote account, visit the Evernote website in your web browser. You can do this on your phone, tablet or computer.

When you get there, look for the link or button to sign up, and click it.

You'll be asked for an e-mail address and a password.

You will use this e-mail address and password on all devices you want to install Evernote on, so make a note of them and keep them safe. Also, if anyone ever wants to share a notebook with you, they'll need your email address, and you need to give them this email address (more on that later).

After entering your details and clicking the sign up button, you will be taken immediately into Evernote Web. It's Evernote, through your browser.

If you go and check your email address, you'll find that Evernote sent you a welcome email, with a download link for Evernote. You can open that email on your phone, tablet or computer, and Evernote will send you to the correct download version for your device.

Download and install Evernote on each device you want to use it on, and then login to Evernote on each device using your email and password specified earlier.

As an alternative to logging in with your email, you can also use your username. This is assigned to you by Evernote when you sign up.

To find your Evernote username, click on your email address in the top right of the screen, and select Account Settings from the menu.

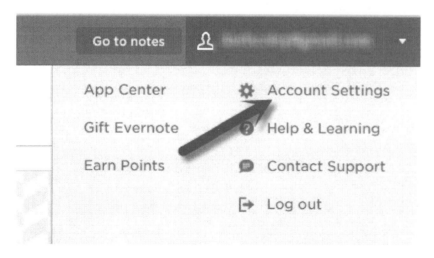

The screen that loads displays your username, which Evernote created from your email address.

You can use that to login instead of your email if you find it easier to remember, or just quicker to type.

Once your account is set up, download the Evernote application for your PC, Mac, tablet or Smartphone, and use those login details to access your account. Your notes will then be synched between all of your devices, no matter which device a note is created on.

How to change your Evernote username

Your username was created automatically from the email address you used when you signed up. There is no way to change this.

How to find your Evernote email address

You actually have two email addresses associated with your Evernote account.

One is the email address you used to sign up for Evernote (the one that you use to login to your account).

The other is an email address assigned to you by Evernote, which allows you to email notes into your account. This email address can be found in your Account Settings.

In Evernote Web, click on your email address (or username) in the top right, and select **Account Settings** from the menu.

One of the entries on that page is **Email Notes to**, which looks like this:

Email Notes to   ▓▓▓▓▓▓▓▓▓▓▓m.evernote.com (?)

Email your notes, snapshots, and audio clips directly into your   Reset
account. Emailed notes will go directly into your default
notebook.

This is the email address you use to send notes via email. We'll look at emailing notes to your Evernote account later in the book.

PC

On the PC version of Evernote, click on the **Tools** menu and select **Account Info**:

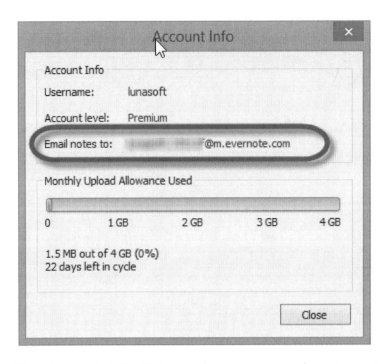

The Account Info dialogue box appears, showing not only your Evernote email address, but also your account level, monthly uploads and days until the next re-bill.

Mac

On a Mac, click the arrow next to your name and select **Account Info** from the drop down menu.

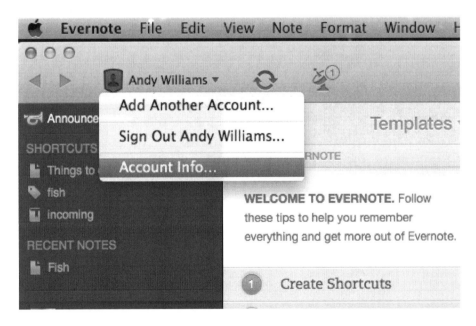

This opens the Account Info screen which displays your Evernote email address.

You can also see your currently month usage and when your next re-bill will occur.

Android

On an Android device, open the sidebar.

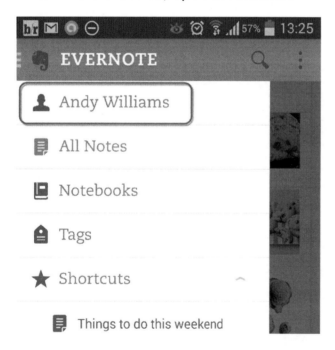

Tap on your name at the top, to open your Account Info screen:

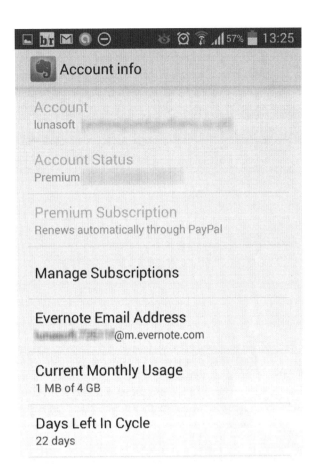

Your Evernote email address is displayed together with other account information, like days left in the billing cycle, monthly usage, etc.

iOS
On the iPad or iPhone open the sidebar.

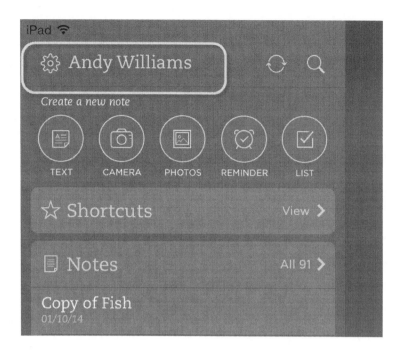

Tap on your name to open up the **Settings** menu.

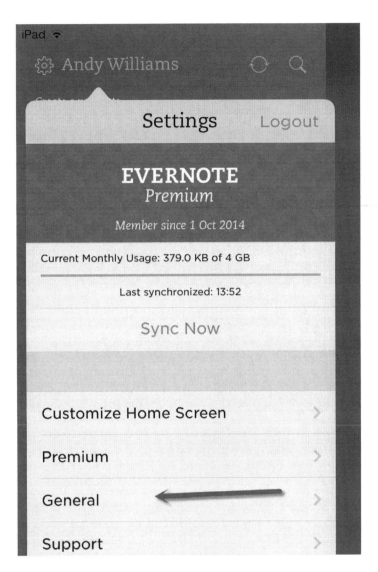

In the settings screen, tap on the General link to open another menu:

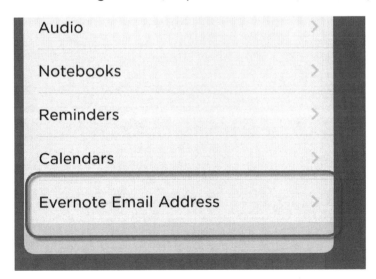

Tap on **Evernote Email Address** to open a screen that displays it.

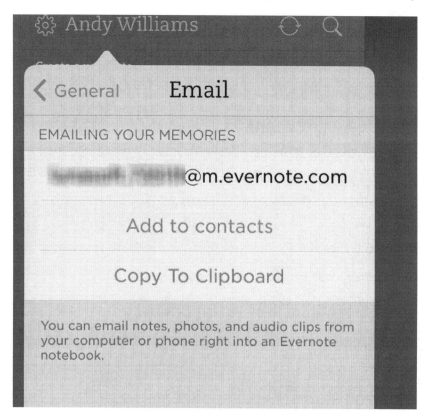

There is a convenient **Copy to Clipboard** link on this screen in case you want to use the email address now.

How to change your Evernote login email address or password

To do this, you'll need to login to Evernote Web (http://evernote.com) using a web browser.

In Evernote Web, click on your name (or email address), top right to access the menu, and click on **Account settings**.

Scroll down until you see the section labeled **Email**. You'll see your email address on the right, with a link to **Manage email addresses**.

Click that link and you'll be taken to the Security Summary screen:

Security Summary

Email Address   davidcoley@gmail.com
                           Change Email

Password   Password last modified in the past 24 hours
                           Change Password

The top option allows you to change your email address, and the second option allows you to change your password. Just click the relevant link and follow the instructions.

Two Step Verification

To do this, you'll need to login to Evernote Web (http://evernote.com) using a web browser.

Two-step verification is an extra layer of safety applied to your Evernote account. Essentially, whenever you login on any device, a verification code is sent to your phone, and you need to enter that, as well as the usual Evernote username and password. If you don't need two-step verification, don't enable it, as it really slows things down.

Still want to enable it?

In Evernote Web, click on your name (or email address), top right to access the menu, and click on **Account settings**.

Scroll down until you see the section labeled **Email**. You'll see your email address on the right, with a link to **Manage email addresses**. Click the link to go to the Security Summary screen.

Security Summary

Email Address	Change Email
Password	Password last modified in the past 24 hours
Change Password
Two-Step Verification	Two-Step Verification is not enabled
Enable

You'll see the option for **Two-Step Verification**, with a link labeled **Enable**. Click the link and follow the instructions to turn it on.

How to close/delete your Evernote account

To do this, you'll need to login to Evernote Web (http://evernote.com) using a web browser.

Evernote allow you to easily deactivate your account, but this will not remove all of your files. They will remain, in case you decide to reactivate later.

Be aware that deactivation does not delete your user login account, so you will not be able to re-register with the same email address.

If you want to deactivate and delete your account content and login information, here are the steps to follow:

1. Contact Evernote Support and tell them you want to delete your account including your email address.
2. If you are a Premium subscriber, cancel the subscription (see next how to for details).
3. In Evernote, delete all of your notes & notebooks. Once you've done that, empty the trash to make sure they are deleted permanently. Now, sync your account so that the deletions are propagated to Evernote's cloud storage.
4. Now it is safe to deactivate your account. To do this, In Evernote Web, click on your name (or email address), top right to access the menu, and click on **Account settings**. Scroll to the bottom of the page, and you'll see a link to **Deactivate your Evernote account**. Click it, and then on the next screen, confirm that you really want to deactivate (check the box and click the button).

How to cancel Evernote Premium or change billing details

To do this, you'll need to login to Evernote Web (http://evernote.com) using a web browser.

If you decide you don't need the Premium subscription any more, you can cancel it via Evernote Web. You can also change the credit card you use for your subscription, or change from monthly to annual or vice versa.

To cancel your Premium subscription, login on the Evernote homepage and click on your name (or email address) top right. Select **Account Settings** from the menu.

On the Accounts Summary tab, there is a section labeled **Billing Summary**.

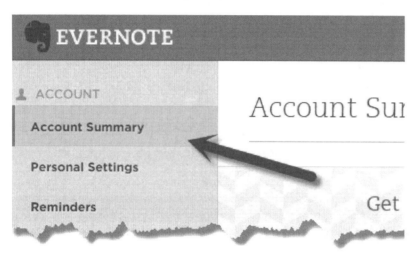

Click on the **Cancel Subscription** option to stop your premium subscription.

If you simply want to change the way you are billed, go to the **Billing info** section.

On this page, you can switch renewal periods or change to a different payment method (iTunes or Amazon subscribers will need to cancel the current subscription before changing payment options).

Interface

Customize Toolbar in desktop versions

The toolbar across the top of Evernote gives you quick access to frequently used features and tasks. However, we all work a little differently, so we may have our own unique requirements for the toolbar. Fortunately, it can be customized on the PC to include the features and tasks we use most often.

PC

Hover your mouse over the toolbar (not over a button in the toolbar, but some white space beside a button), and right click your mouse:

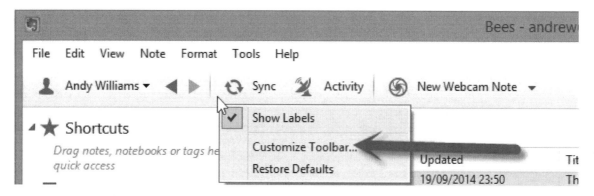

A menu appears with an option to **Customize Toolbar..**

Click it to open the toolbar editor.

The editor contains a grid of buttons that you can include in your toolbar if you want to. Simply drag and drop buttons to and from your toolbar to add or remove them.

When you have the toolbar as you want it, click the **Done** button to save.

Mac

Previous versions of Evernote for Mac allowed customizations to the toolbar, but the latest version does not seem to. They may add this back at some point in the future, but for now you are stuck with the toolbar they gave you.

Customize what shows in the left sidebar on desktop versions

Evernote can show a lot of stuff in the left sidebar, and on the PC and Mac, you can customize what is shown.

PC

From the View menu at the top, select **Left Panel** to open up a checklist of options:

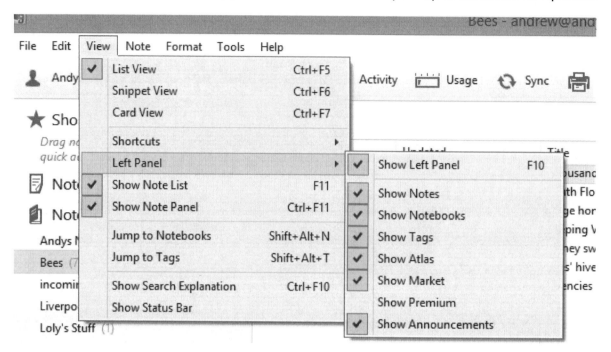

The top option allows you to hide the left panel altogether (function key F10 will also do this).

While that is not something most people will want to do, we can turn the following on or off by checking /unchecking the option:

- Notes
- Notebooks
- Tags
- Atlas
- Market
- Premium
- Announcements

Check only those items that you want displayed in your sidebar.

Mac

On a Mac, you can modify what is shown in the left sidebar from the **View** menu at the top.

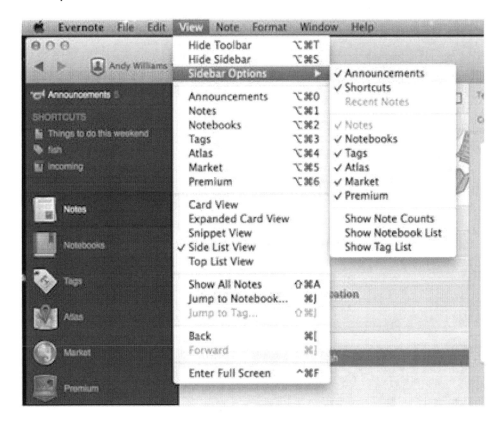

At the top of the View menu, you can hide the sidebar altogether (or show it if it is already hidden). You can do the same with the toolbar.

The sidebar options are the third item in the menu, and that opens up a sub-menu.

Place a check mark (this is toggled by clicking) next to the items you want to show in the sidebar.

At the bottom of the Sidebar Options menu, you have a few more options. You can choose to show a Note count, notebook list and tag list in the sidebar.

If you don't have Notebooks visible in the sidebar, Evernote for Mac will only show **Notebooks** as a single entry, and clicking on that opens up a screen listing all notebooks.

If you choose to show notebooks in the sidebar, Evernote will list them all there for quick access.

I've also added note counts for that screenshot (see the numbers after the notebook name), and the tag list (see below the notebooks section).

Android

On Android devices, the only customization you can do with the sidebar is to show/hide two sections – **Market** and **Explore Evernote**.

To toggle these on or off, enter the settings menu (tap the three vertical dots in the top right of the screen, then tap **Settings**).

Scroll down the settings until you get to **Navigation** and tap on it.

You have check boxes to show/hide these two sections on the sidebar.

iOS
On the iPad, click open the sidebar.

Now click on your name, top left, or the little cog to the left of your name.

The Settings screen will open, and the top menu item is **Customize Home Screen**.

Tap this to open a menu with lots of settings you can change. Here is the top part of that menu:

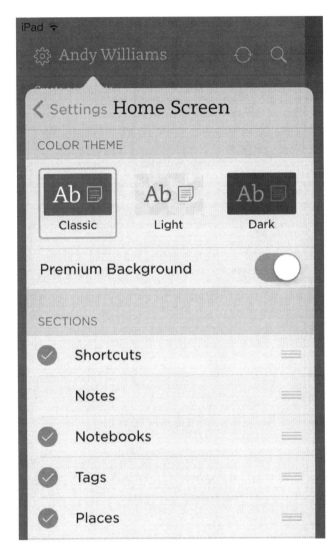

At the very top, you can change the **color theme** used by Evernote on your iPad.

Lower down the Home screen, you have a list of the sections displayed in the sidebar. You can drag the various sections around to reorder them. Tap and hold the three horizontal lines to the right of an item you want to move, and drag up or down to the desired location before dropping.

You can also toggle these sections on or off by tapping the check mark next to them, but people with big fingers will probably find this quite difficult, especially on an iPad mini or iPhone.

The lower part of the menu is shown below:

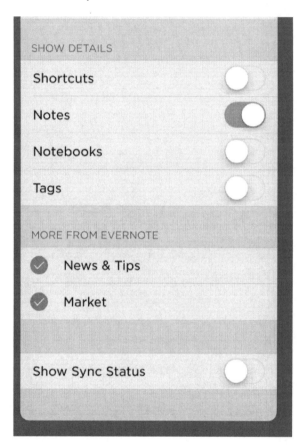

The **Show Details** section determines whether or not that section is expanded or collapsed.

For example, in the screenshot above, Notes is active (expanded), so the notes section of my sidebar will be open, showing a few of the more recently active/updated notes.

I can also expand the notebooks or tags in a similar way. Expanded, these sections show the most recently active items in those sections.

At the bottom of this menu, you can turn off **News & Tips** and **Market** so they don't appear as sections of your sidebar.

Finally, you can choose to show or hide the sync status in the sidebar.

Creating Notes

Since notes are the main heart and soul of Evernote, you need to know how to create them. This is actually very easy, but it is different on different platforms, so let's take a look at each in turn, starting with Evernote Web (login at Evernote.com).

You can't really miss the large **New Note** button in the toolbar at the top, so there really isn't too much to say, other than, your new note will be created in whichever Notebook is currently selected in the left sidebar. If no notebook is selected, the note will be created in your default notebook.

In this screenshot:

If I tap on the **New Note** button, my new note is created in the **Bees** notebook.

When you add a note, it will open in Evernote, ready for editing:

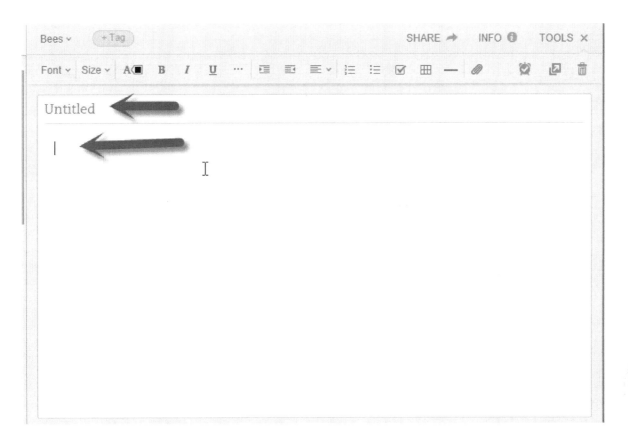

Firstly, click into the large white rectangle that will hold the body of your note. When you do, the editing & formatting toolbar appears.

At the very top left of the note, you can see the word **Bees**. This is the notebook that the note is in. Clicking on the word **Bees** will open a list of all notebooks, which can be selected to move the note to a different notebook.

Next to this in the toolbar is a list of tags assigned to the note. In this case, there are none, because the note is new. If you want to add tags, click into this area and start typing.

You will also see the buttons Share, Info and Tools, which we'll look at later.

The editing toolbar allows you to format text, add images, attach files, use checkboxes, bullets or numbered lists. Everything you need to create richly formatted notes.

You can give each note a title by typing where it currently says **Untitled**.

OK, so where is the Save button?

Well, there isn't one.

You'll get used to this as you use Evernote. Everything is saved frequently, so you won't lose anything. The lack of a save button can be disconcerting for new users, but trust me, your data is safe. Concentrate on your notes, and let Evernote worry about saving it.

OK, so that's Evernote Web. Let's look at Evernote on the PC.

PC

You'll find the **New Note** button in the toolbar at the top.

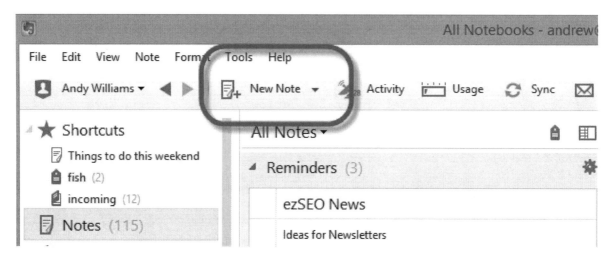

It is possible to edit this toolbar, only displaying button you want to show, so if that button is not there, chances are you've been playing around and removed it. Just check out the section of this book on customizing the toolbar and you can add it back.

Now, the **New Note** button can be used in two ways. The clue to its double life is the small downward pointing arrow to the right of the **New Note** text.

If you click on the **New Note** button (not on the arrow side), a new note will be created for you. If you have a notebook selected in the left sidebar, the note will be created in that notebook. If no notebook is selected, your new note will be created in the default notebook.

In the following screenshot, I had my Recipes notebook open when I click the **New Note** button:

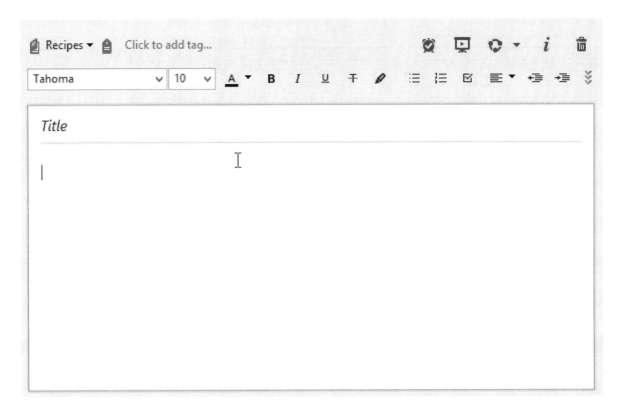

At the very top left of the note, you can see the word **Recipes**. That's the notebook the note is in. There is a drop down arrow on that notebook button, and you can click it and select a different notebook if you want to move the note.

Next to the notebook, you'll see the tags assigned to the note. In this case, none as it is new. If you **Click to add tag**... that area becomes editable and you can type in a tag.

Over on the right of the top toolbar, you can see some more buttons. These allow you to set reminders, share notes, etc. Again, we'll see those options later in the book.

Below this top toolbar you can see the note formatting options. If you don't see this lower toolbar, click into the large rectangle that will hold the body of your note, and it will appear.

On the far right, you may see a "chevron", which drops down a menu showing any items in the toolbar that are missing through lack of screen width. Here are those items on my screen:

Those four buttons allow you to add a table, horizontal line, a file attachment and an audio recording.

OK, remember that I told you the **New Note** button lead a double life? Well, click the arrow to the right of the **New Note** text:

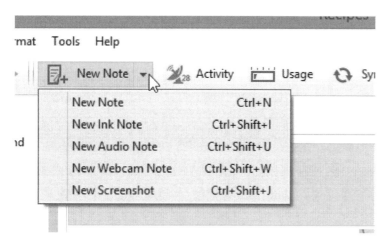

This button allows you to create specific types of notes. The top option is a normal text note, followed by Ink note (hand-written), audio, webcam and screenshot.

If you want to, play around with the different note types. When you finish playing, you can use the delete button on the note toolbar to delete those you don't want to keep.

Mac

In the toolbar at the top of Evernote, you'll see a **New Note** button. The label on that button will depend on what you've been up to. For example, I've selected my Bees notebook from the left sidebar, and this is the new note button I see:

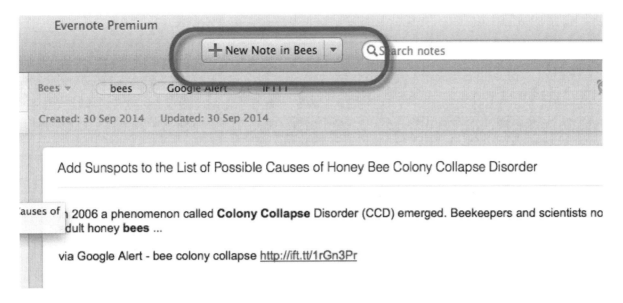

It's offering to add a new note into the Bees notebook. This makes sense, since that is the notebook I am working in.

If I click the arrow on the right of this button, I get more options

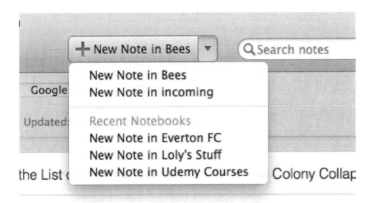

At the top of this menu, it offers to add a new note in my currently selected notebook, which is the same as just clicking the New Note button without this menu.

Underneath, it offers to add a new note to **Incoming**. Incoming is the name of my default notebook. Your default notebook may be called something else, so that name will be used there.

You then have a section that lists recently open notebooks. You can quickly add a new note to any of these by clicking on the menu item.

But what if you want to add a note to a notebook that isn't listed in this menu?

If you have the notebooks visible in the left sidebar, click on the one you want to add the note to, and then click the **New Note** button.

If you do not have the notebooks visible in the sidebar, you can click on **Notebooks** and get a list of notebooks displayed. You can then click the one you want to add the note to, and the **New Note** button will update to say **New Note in...** whichever notebook you selected.

Of course, if you create a new note and then decide to move it to another notebook, that is easy too.

Just click the Notebook menu top left, and select the notebook you want to move it to:

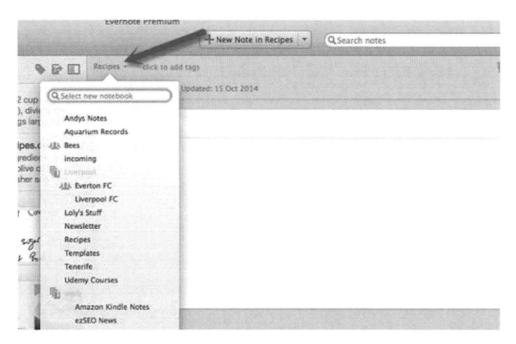

When you add a new note in Evernote for Mac, it opens ready for editing:

If you click into the large rectangle where the body of your note will be, the toolbars appear above the note.

The top toolbar lists the notebook the note is in (Recipes in my screenshot), which you can change as we saw a moment ago. You then have a list of tags, in this case none because it is a new note (you can click into the toolbar to add tags). On the right of the top toolbar, you can buttons to create a reminder, share, create a presentation, delete note, etc.

The lower toolbar is the formatting toolbar. This one allows you to format your notes, and add an audio recording, snapshot or file attachment.

You can play around with these options if you like. We will look at them later. When you've finished playing around, delete any notes you do not want using the trash can button in the toolbar.

Android
The Evernote for Android interface has been going through some changes, and one change I particularly like is the way you add new notes.

On opening Evernote, you'll see the **Add Note** button bottom right:

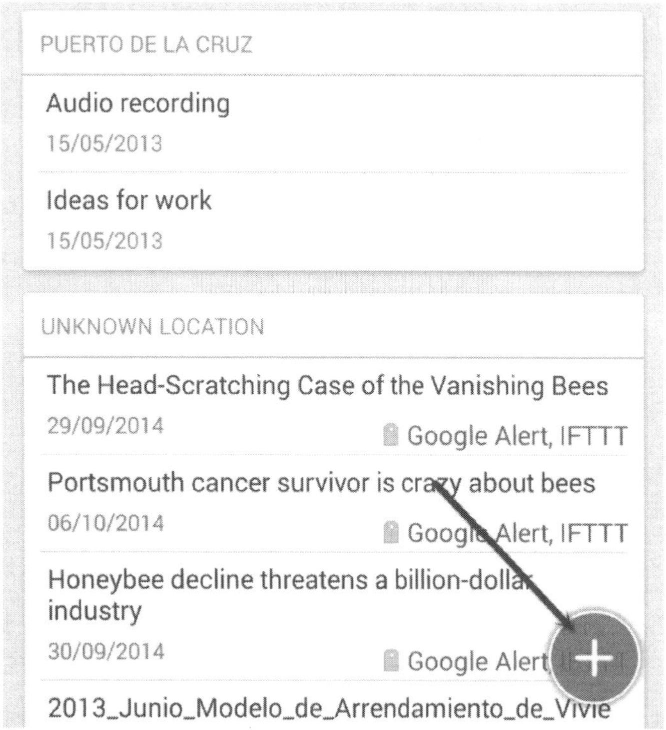

PUERTO DE LA CRUZ

Audio recording
15/05/2013

Ideas for work
15/05/2013

UNKNOWN LOCATION

The Head-Scratching Case of the Vanishing Bees
29/09/2014   🔖 Google Alert, IFTTT

Portsmouth cancer survivor is crazy about bees
06/10/2014   🔖 Google Alert, IFTTT

Honeybee decline threatens a billion-dollar industry
30/09/2014   🔖 Google Alert, IFTTT

2013_Junio_Modelo_de_Arrendamiento_de_Vivie

Tap it to open a lovely little menu:

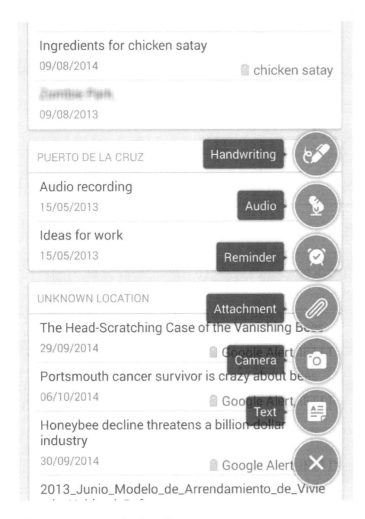

This menu includes buttons you can tap to add handwritten notes, audio notes, reminders, attachments, photos from the camera or basic text notes.

Once you've added a note, or indeed go in to edit an existing one, you'll see this button in the bottom right corner:

☐ Newsletter. Review call to action pro.

☐ Start putting recipes in book.

☐ Cover for multiplication drills.

$A^{\equiv}$

Tapping that opens the formatting menu:

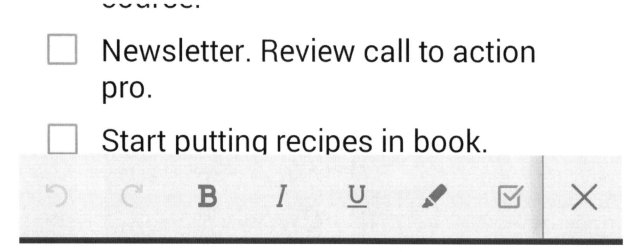

This menu includes bold, italics, underline, a highlighting pen (which takes some getting used to) and the option for adding checkboxes.

Go on, play around a little.

If you are working in a notebook, adding a new note will add it to that notebook. If you are not working in any particular notebook, the new note is added to your default notebook.

iOS

On iOS devices, you can add notes in a couple of different ways.

The first is to open the sidebar and use the buttons just under your name:

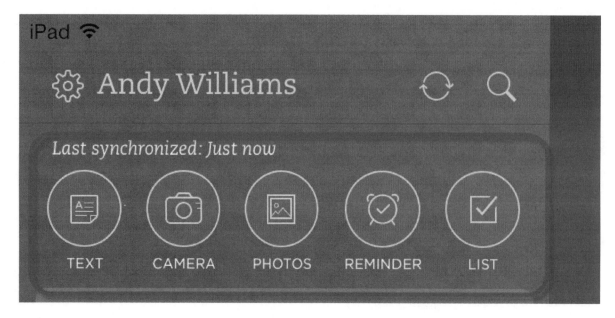

These buttons will add a text note, camera snapshot, photos from your camera roll, reminder and list type note.

When you tap one of these buttons, your new note is added to your default notebook, but it is easy enough to move.

On tapping a button, the new note is displayed on the screen for editing:

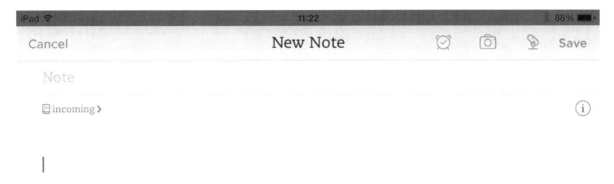

If you decide you actually don't want to create the note, tap the **Cancel** button (top left).

If you want to move it to another notebook, you can tap the notebook icon (mine is labeled as "incoming"), to be offered a scrollable list of all notebooks, and simply tap the one you want to move the note to.

On the top right of the **New Note** screen, you can see some buttons. These are to add a reminder, a photo and an audio recording. You've also got a save button for when you finish editing the note. Having an actual **save** button in Evernote is unusual, since saving is all automatic. That button simply tells Evernote you are finished editing. To be more in line with Evernote on other platforms, that button might better be labeled "Done".

Also on the **New Note** screen, you can see a small circle with the letter "i" inside. We will look at that later in the book, but if you want a sneak peek, tap it now.

Changing the way notes are displayed

The list of notes in Evernote can be displayed in different formats, depending on platform.

PC

On the PC, you can change the way notes are displayed via the **View** menu.

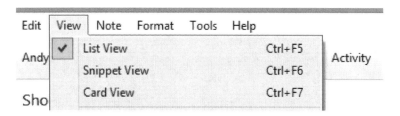

There are three options to choose from.

Option 1 is "List view":

Created	Updated	Title	Notebook	Tags
19/09/2014 23:50	19/09/2014 23:50	Thousands of honey bees killed, hive destr...	Bees	Google
19/09/2014 23:50	19/09/2014 23:50	South Florida beekeepers stress importance...	Bees	Google
19/09/2014 23:50	19/09/2014 23:50	Large honeybee hive destroyed	Bees	Google
18/09/2014 21:29	18/09/2014 21:29	Keeping Virginia Bees Buzzing	Bees	Google
19/09/2014 23:50	19/09/2014 23:50	Honey sweetens Rosh Hashanah, despite to...	Bees	Google
19/09/2014 15:28	19/09/2014 15:28	Bees' hive of action a must	Bees	Google
19/09/2014 06:48	19/09/2014 06:48	Agencies meet for close-up look at whethe...	Bees	Google

Option 2 is **Snippet View:**

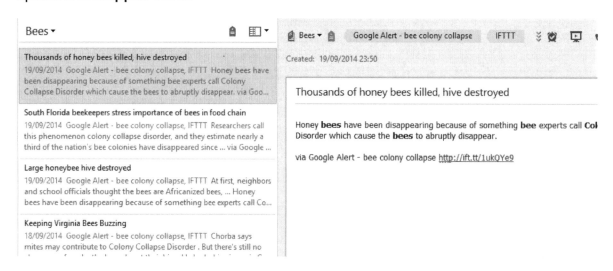

In this view, each note includes a short excerpt, with the full note being shown to the right.

Option 3 is the card view:

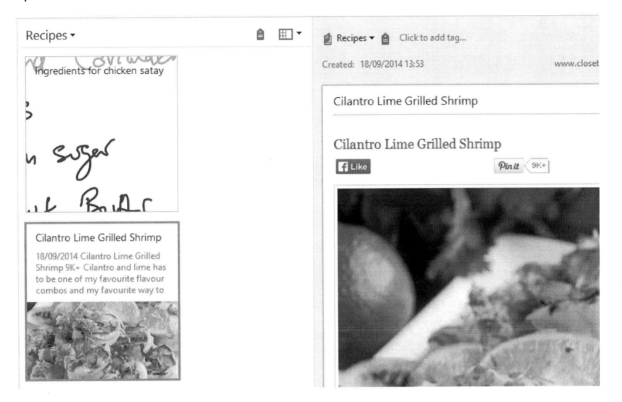

This view shows each note as a small card, again with the full note to the right. Each card shows a small part of the note.

Mac

On a Mac, click on a Notebook in the left sidebar. All of the notes in that notebook appear in the column to the right. How they appear depends on how you have Evernote set up.

In the following screenshot, I've got them displaying as **Side List View**:

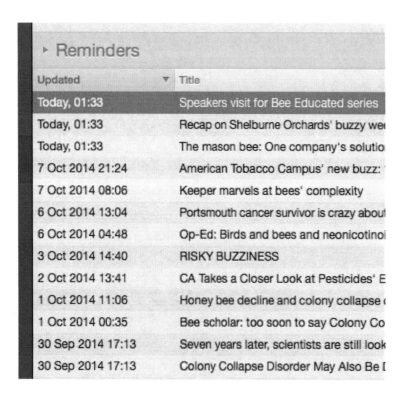

Evernote for Mac offers 5 different display options, available via the small **View Options** button top right:

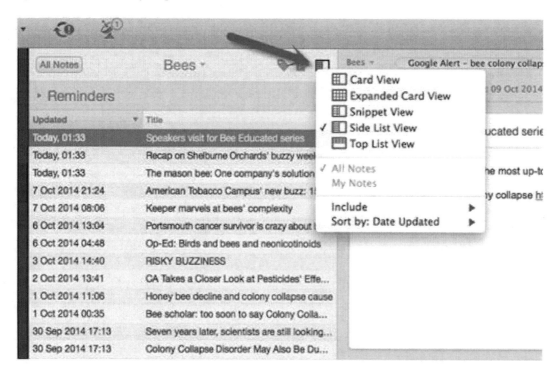

Click a view option to select it.

Here are screenshots of the other four display modes available:

Card View:

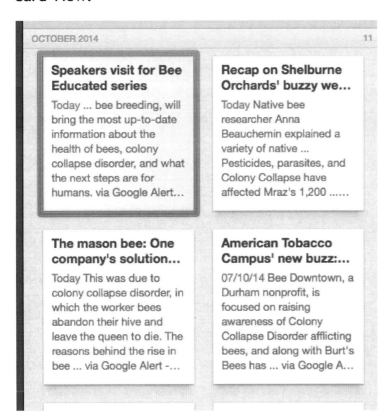

Cards are arranged in two columns, and clicking on one displays that note in the panel to the right.

Expanded Card View:

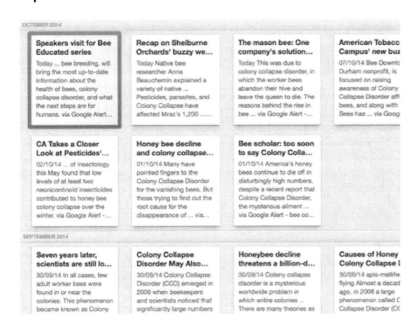

This view takes up the full screen, with cards stretching across the full width of Evernote. To view a note in this view, double click it. It will open in a new window.

Snippet View:

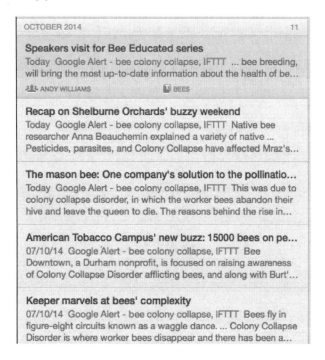

This is similar to the Side list view, but each note includes a small excerpt. Clicking on one of these items displays the whole note in the panel to the right.

Top List View:

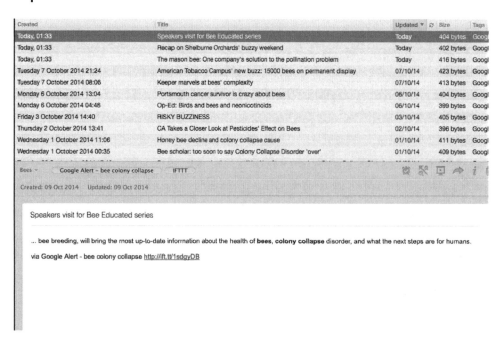

This view splits the screen into an upper and lower section. In the upper section, you have a list of all notes. In the lower section, you can see the currently selected note, in full.

Android
There is only one view of notes, and it cannot be changed on Android.

iOS
There is only one view of notes, and it cannot be changed on iOS.

Access Evernote Options screen

The Evernote options controls how the program works, so it is important to be able to find them.

I'll give you a very brief overview of what settings can be changed in the options, but I recommend you go in and have a look around to familiarize yourself with them.

PC

On a PC, click the **Tools** menu and select **Options** from the menu. The options are spread across several tabs:

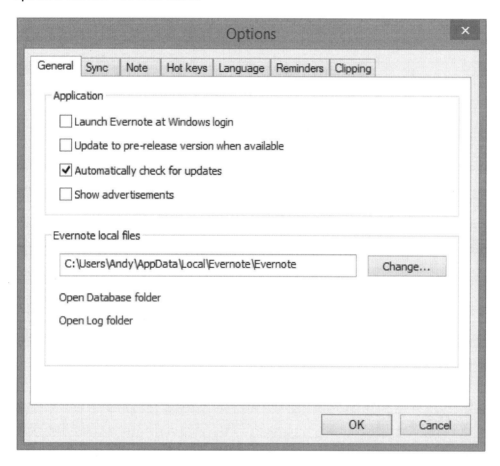

The General tab controls the basic behavior of the application. You can choose to launch Evernote when Windows starts, auto-check for updates and to show/hide advertisements. You can also change where local files are stored on your computer.

The Sync tab controls how Evernote Syncs, including the frequency.

The Note tab allows you to change the font (and size) used in the note editor, as well as how Evernote should handle PDF files attached to notes.

The Hot Keys tab allows you to set up hotkey combinations for tasks like adding a new note, searching, copying and pasting.

The Language tab allows you to change the default language used in the application, as well as the language you want to use for spell checking. You can select an option here to check spelling as you type, which is useful because misspelled words will have a squiggly line underneath, and right clicking the word opens a menu with suggestions on the correct spelling.

The Reminders tab offers you the option of receiving an email when reminders are triggered. If you choose to have the emails delivered, be aware that these are delivered on the morning when the reminder is due, not at the specific time the reminder is set to be triggered.

Finally, the Clipping tab allows you to set a default notebook for incoming clips as well as a few other clipping options.

Mac

In the Mac version of Evernote, the options are called Preferences, as is the convention on Mac computers. You will find the options in the Evernote application menu. Alternatively, you can press the command key with the comma.

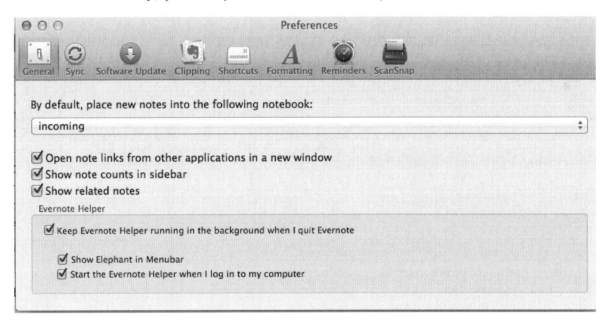

On the **General** tab, you can choose the default notebook as well as a few other options which you can see in the screenshot above.

On the **Sync** tab, you can change the time between syncs. Default is every 15 minutes.

The **Software Update** tab allows you to decide how Evernote application updates are installed. You can choose to have Evernote automatically check for updates, and install them, or you might decide you want to manually check and update. You can also choose to install Evernote beta versions when they are ready (for those that like living on the edge).

The **Clipping** tab allows you to tell Evernote how you want to handle clippings that are sent to Evernote. You can also download the Evernote Web Clipper from that screen.

The **Shortcuts** tab allows you to define global keyboard shortcuts for controlling Evernote.

The **Formatting** tab allows you to set the default fonts used for note text, and how the date should be formatted. You can also choose to have formatting simplified when items are pasted into a note.

The **Reminders** tab allows you to "opt in" to receiving an email notification on the morning a reminder is due.

The **ScanSnap** tab is for those that want to use the ScanSnap device with Evernote.

Android
There is no equivalent Options screen on the Android version. All of the settings are available in the Setting menu, accessible by tapping the three vertical dots top right, and selecting Settings from the menu.

iOS
There is no equivalent Options screen on the iPad. All configurable options are found in the Setting menu, accessible by tapping the elephant icon top left, then tapping your name, or the small cog to the left of your name. This opens the settings menu which contains a few sub-menus.

Syncing

How to sync Evernote between devices

The beauty of Evernote is that you can have your notes on all of your computers, tablets & phones, and these are always kept in sync with each other. The first thing you need to do (obviously), is to download and install Evernote on each of your devices. Login to each one using your email address and password. From now on, anything created or deleted on one device will be synced to all of your other devices running Evernote on the same Evernote account.

Syncing of the notes between devices will be done automatically, at specified intervals. These intervals are determined by the setting in the options we saw earlier. However, you can sync manually as well.

PC
On a PC, you can see the automatic sync interval in the Sync options:

Mine is set to every 30 minutes.

However, if you want to sync manually because you need something shared quickly on your other devices, you can manually sync in a few different ways.

1. Clicking the **Sync** button in the toolbar (if you haven't removed it when customizing the toolbar).
2. Pressing F9 function key on your keyboard.
3. Clicking on Sync in the Tools menu.

Mac

On the Mac, open the Preferences screen (from the Evernote application menu, or Command key plus comma). Click onto the Sync tab:

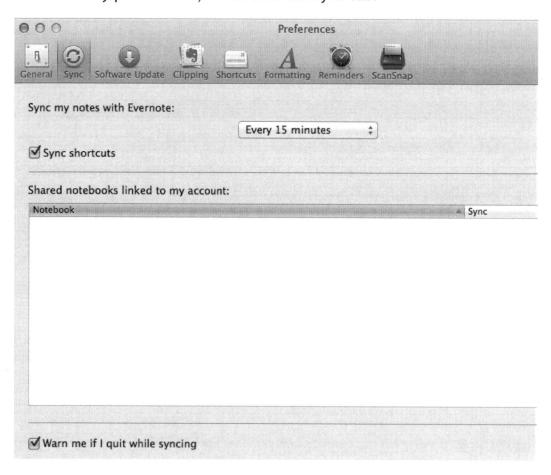

The default setting is for Evernote to Sync every 15 minutes, but you can click on that to change the value. Options include every 5, 15, 30 minutes, or every hour. Alternatively you can select to sync **Manually**, which turns off automatic syncing.

You can always manually sync your notes whenever you want, by looking for, and clicking the **Sync** button in the toolbar:

The keyboard shortcut for syncing is:

CTRL + Command + s

Android

On Android devices, you can manually sync by clicking the Sync item in the main menu (tap the three vertical dots).

You can also control how Evernote automatically syncs.

Go to the Settings menu and scroll down until you get to the **General Settings** section. Click on **Sync** to open this screen:

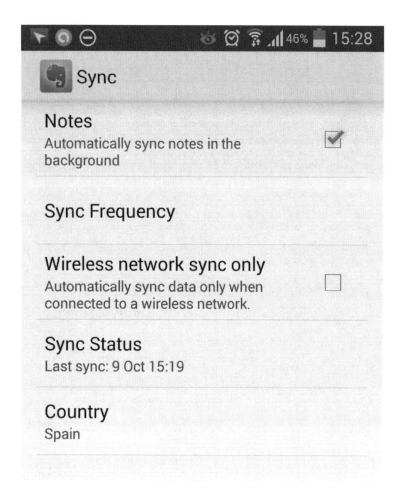

The top option is checked, and this turns automatic syncing on. Uncheck to turn it off.

Tapping on **Sync Frequency** will give you a list of frequencies to choose from: Every 15, 30, 60 minutes, or every day.

Back on the Sync screen, you can see that I have **Wireless network sync only** unchecked. Check this option if you want Evernote to only sync when connected to a WIFI connection (and never when using your 3G/4G data connection).

iOS

At the top of the left sidebar there is a sync button which you can use any time you want to manually sync your notes.

There are no settings in the iOS version to allow you to change the frequency of syncing, but syncing will automatically occur every few minutes, and when you start Evernote.

CloudHQ for Power Syncing

Disclaimer: I have never used CloudHQ and have no association with them. They just seem like a really cool service, and one that a lot of Evernote users might find useful.

CloudHQ is a paid service that will allow you to sync between a lot of different platforms, including Evernote, Google Drive, Gmail, Dropbox, OneDrive, Basecamp plus others.

CloudHQ can backup and sync Evernote with all of these services. It allows you to consolidate documents from each service, so they are available to all services.

For example, if you make a change in Google Docs, you can access it from Dropbox, Evernote, etc.

If this sounds interesting, you can check out their website.

https://www.cloudhq.net/evernote

Backing Up & Archiving

Backups or just sync

Backups are important on computers and digital devices in case of a disaster. Most of the time, a disaster usually consists of a device failure, and inability to access the hard drive or storage medium containing your data.

In the case of Evernote, it's a little different, since anything on your device is stored in the cloud, and if your device fails, you simply install Evernote on another device, use the same login details and your data is still there. There is one exception to this – local notebooks.

Local notebooks are only stored on the device you create them on, so are not synced with the Evernote cloud. That means, if your device fails, you lose your local notebooks!

For those that want to backup, let's look at the backup options.

How to backup/export Evernote notes

Backups can be done on PCs and Mac, but not mobile versions of Evernote.

PC

We have two options for backing up Evernote data. The first is done using Evernote itself, and the other is done by backing up the local files in the folder where Evernote stores your data.

Option 1 – Using Evernote

To backup using Evernote, we can create an Evernote archive file. These have .enex file extensions, and can be used to restore your notes if you ever need to.

To backup all of your data, right click on **Notebooks** in the left sidebar and select **Export Notes**. You'll be offered different ways to backup, but I suggest you stick with the ENEX format so that it can be easily restored later if needed.

NOTE: To backup a single notebook, right click on the notebook you want to backup and only that notebook will be exported. This is useful if you want to archive old notebooks (see later).

You'll see an **Options** button on the **Export** screen, and this allows you to specify exactly what is backed up, but assuming you want a full backup, leave everything checked on the **Export Options** screen.

When you click on the Export button, you'll be asked where you want to create the backup file, so select a destination and proceed with the backup. You'll get a message saying the backup was successful. OK, that's option 1. Keep your backup safe.

Option 2 - Backing Evernote local data files

To backup the local data files (consisting of all your data), you need to know where Evernote stores your database. To find this, open the **Options** screen from the **Tools** menu. On the **General** tab, you'll see the location of Evernote local files:

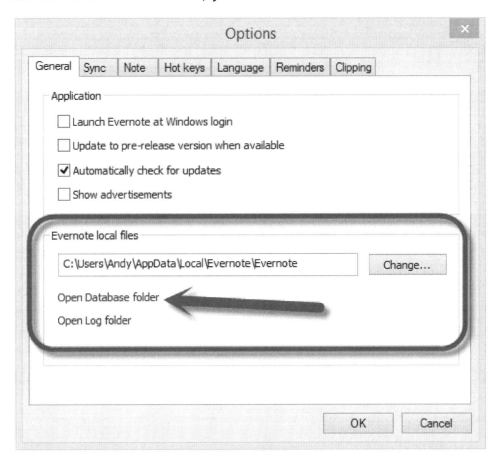

However, this is not the folder you want to backup. What you need to backup is the **Database** folder. It will be the above folder with "/databases" added to the end. There is a link to this folder on the **General** options tab (see above). Click it to open the databases folder in Windows File Explorer.

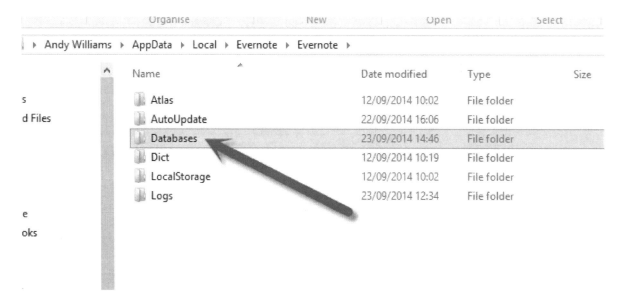

It is this "databases" folder you need to backup.

If you need a good backup program to automate backups, I recommend one called GoodSync. You can see my review of it here:

http://andyjwilliams.co.uk/technology/windows-8-woes/

Mac

To backup notes, we need to select the notes for backup before issuing the backup command.

If you want to backup all notes in your account, click on **Notebooks** in the left sidebar. This selects all of your notes.

If you want to backup all notes in a notebook, click on that notebook in the left sidebar, then press Command + A to select all notes.

You can also backup only those notes that meet a search enquiry. Do the search, then Command + A to select them all for backup.

Alternatively, you can Command + Click to select individual notes in the list, or Shift + click to select sequential notes in the list.

When all notes are selected, choose **Export Notes** from the File menu. If you selected **Notebooks** to backup all notes, this will say **Export All Notes...** instead. A dialogue box opens, asking how and where to save the exported notes:

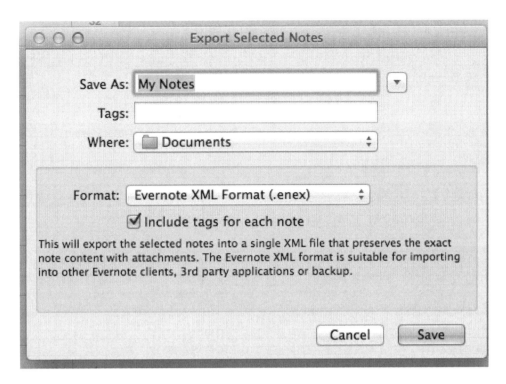

You can choose a name for your backup file and add some tags to all exported notes, and specify a location.

Under format, the default option is **Evernote XML format (.enex)**, and I suggest you choose that unless you have good reason for wanting an HTML export (which is the other option).

The checkbox under format determines whether or not you want the tags used by these notes exported as well. Check it if you do, uncheck if you don't.

When you are ready, click **Save** and your notes will be exported.

This file can be used to restore your notes if you ever need to (see the next "how to").

How to Restore Evernote Backups

OK, you've got your backups somewhere safe, so let's see how you can restore your data from one of these backups. This can be done on Mac or PC.

PC

If you took an ENEX backup (option 1 in the previous section), then you can restore the file within Evernote.

From the **File** menu, click on **Import** then select **Evernote Export Files...**

A dialogue box opens asking where your backup file is located.

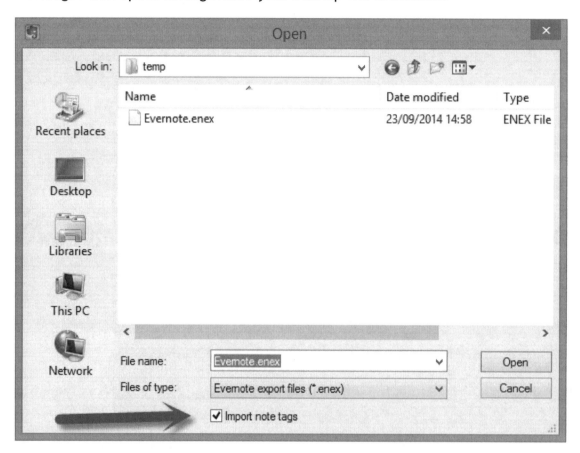

Note that if you want tags to be imported (assuming they were exported in the first place), make sure the checkbox **Import note tags** is checked.

Select your backup and click OK.

You'll get a confirmation screen that asks if you want to add the notes into a synchronized notebook. I recommend you select **No** to save upload quota until you are happy with the way your notes are arranged. Read on and this will make more sense.

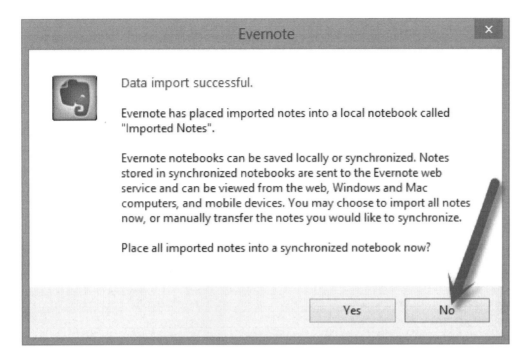

Evernote creates a new Notebook called **Imported Notes** with all of your data.

You can now create Notebooks to move the imported notes to a better home. Once all notes are moved to the correct Notebooks, delete the **Imported Notes** notebook.

If you backed up Evernote data by backing up the database folder, simply re-install Evernote and then close it down. Now copy the Database backup folder, back into the Evernote local data folder, over-writing the existing databases folder. Restart Evernote and your data will be restored.

Mac

Hopefully you have your notes backed up carefully in the ENEX format. We saw how to do this in the previous "how to".

From the File menu, select **Import Notes**. The **Import Notes Archive** screen opens:

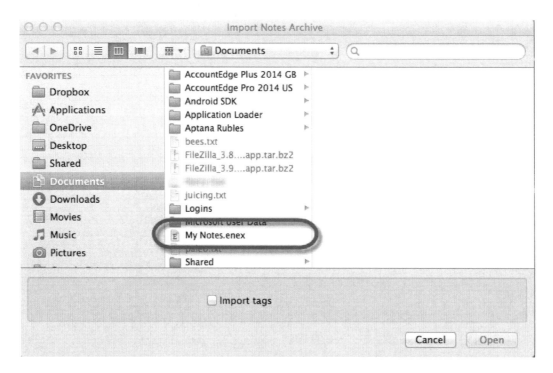

Navigate to your backup file, select it, and click **Open**.

All of the notes in the archive will be imported. These notes are imported into a local notebook. Here is the explanation from Evernote:

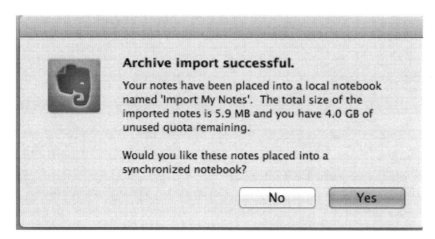

The dialogue asks if you want the notes imported into a synchronized notebook. I would recommend you select **No**.

Placing them into a synchronized notebook would start all of the notes uploading to Evernote servers, something you probably don't want just yet (think about your upload bandwidth limits on your Evernote account). By selecting **No**, you can sort through the notes, and manually move them to existing notebooks, or create new notebooks to house them. Once all notes have been re-housed, delete the **Import My Notes** local notebook (right click it in the left sidebar and choose **Delete**).

How to archive Evernote notebooks

Unfortunately, Evernote does not have an archive feature at the moment. They might add one in the future, and I'd suggest they need to if they are going to keep long-term customers happy.

The idea of archiving is simple. Some notes or notebooks become less important to us, but we don't want to delete them. An archiving system would allow use to move those notebooks to an archive where they would not be involved in searches, unless you specifically want to search the archived notebooks.

The only real option (which is not ideal) is to create a local backup the notebook as an ENEX file. Then you can safely delete the notebook from within Evernote. You won't be able to search these backups, but if you ever need the notebook again, you can re-import it.

For instructions on creating these notebook backups, see the earlier "How to" on creating backups.

Working with Notebooks

How to create a Notebook – sync or local

Notes are stored in notebooks, and the more specific your notebooks, the better organized your notes will be. Fortunately, creating notebooks is very easy. However, be aware that notebooks are either local or synchronized, and you cannot change this setting once the notebook has been created.

PC

Go to the File menu, and click on **New Notebook**.

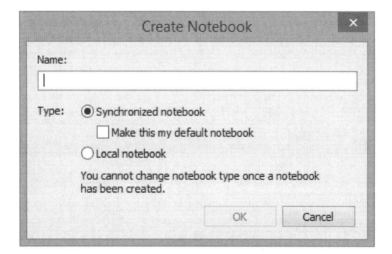

Enter a name for your notebook, and decide whether the notebook should be synchronized or local. If it is synchronized, you can also make it your default notebook by checking the **Make this my default notebook** option.

Click OK to create the notebook.

Another way of creating a new notebook, is to simply right click on the left sidebar on an existing notebook and select **Create Notebook**. You'll get the same Create Notebook dialogue as we saw a moment ago.

Mac

If you click on Notebooks in the left sidebar, you'll see a button at the top labeled **New Notebook**. This button will always create synchronized notebooks. If that is what you want, then this is one way to achieve that.

The other way to create a new Notebook is via the **File** menu.

Clicking on **New Notebook** opens a menu asking if you want a Synchronized Notebook or a Local Notebook. Choose wisely, since you cannot change this later.

Once you have created a new notebook, click on **Notebooks** in the left sidebar and all of your notebooks are listed. Mouse over your new notebook (or any of them for that matter), and you'll see two icons appear:

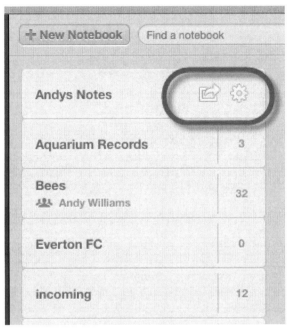

The first icon is to **Share** or **Publish** this notebook. We'll look at that later.

The second option opens up the notebook settings:

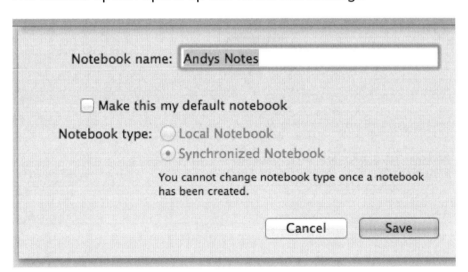

As you can see, you cannot change the notebook type. If it was created as a synchronized notebook, it will stay as a synchronized notebook. If it was made local, it stays local (see later for a work-around for this problem). What you can do on this screen is to make a notebook your default notebook. Your default notebook is where notes will be created by default, unless you specifically tell Evernote to use a different notebook.

Android

To create a new notebook on your Android device, pull out the left sidebar and tap Notebooks to take you to the notebooks screen.

At the top of the screen, you'll see a **New Notebook** button:

Click this button and you'll be prompted to enter a name for the notebook.

Your new notebook will be created as a synchronized notebook. You cannot create a local notebook on Android.

In addition, you cannot delete a notebook on Android.

iOS

Open the left sidebar and tap on notebooks.

At the top, you'll see a button to add a **New Notebook**. Tap it and you'll be prompted for a title.

Creating a notebook on an iPad will only create synchronized notebooks. You cannot create a local one.

You can delete a notebook on iOS, unlike on Android where this is not an option.

On your iPad, open the left sidebar again and tap **Notebooks** to open the list of notebooks.

At the top of this screen, on the right, you'll see a link to **Edit**. Tap it.

All of the notebooks will have a new button in front of the name, which will delete that notebook.

After the name, there are two icons.

The first allows you to **Share** the notebook with other people via email.

The second button opens up the information screen for that notebook, allowing you to rename the notebook, add it to your shortcuts, make available offline (if you are a Premium user), add the notebook to a stack, or delete the notebook.

How to move a local notebook to sync or vice

When you create a new notebook, you have to choose between local or synced. The problem is that there is no way to change this once it is set up. A synced notebook will always be synced and a local will always be local.

There is a work-around.

If you want to move from synced to local, create a new local notebook.

If you want to move from local to synced, create a new synced notebook.

You cannot name the new notebook with the same name as the one you want to change, but this is not important as the name can be changed later.

Now, drag the notes from the original notebook, into the newly created one. Once all notes are moved, delete the old notebook. If you want to change the name of your new notebook to match the old notebook name, right click on the notebook and select properties. You have the option to change the name.

How to create a stack

As we saw earlier, a stack is a "pile" of related notebooks. You can easily create stacks.

PC

Simply drag and drop one notebook onto another one. Evernote will create the stack.

The stack will be labeled as **Notebook Stack** and then **Notebook Stack [2]** if you create another one. Once a stack is created, right click on **Notebook Stack**, and select **Rename**:

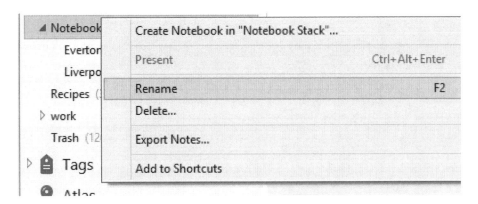

You can then give it a more meaningful name:

To remove notebooks from a stack, simply drag and drop the notebook on top of **Notebooks**.

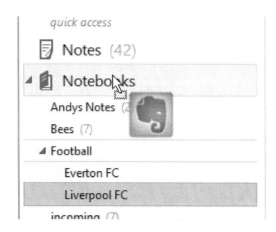

Or you can drop it onto another notebook if you want to add it to (or create) a different stack.

If you drag all notebooks out of a stack, the stack will disappear.

Mac
Click on **Notebooks** in the left sidebar.

Your notebooks appear in a vertical list to the right of the sidebar. To create a new stack, simply click and drag one notebook on top of another, then release it. The stack will be created using the name of the notebook that was receiving the one you dragged and dropped.

As you drag one notebook on top of another, you'll notice a rectangle appear around the one that will receive the dropped notebook:

Once you drop the notebook, the stack is shown as a single rectangle, with a number inside, referring to the number of notebooks in that stack:

Double click a stack to see its contents:

To remove a notebook from a stack, drag and drop it into the background space above or below the stack:

Android
Bring out the left sidebar and tap on Notebooks.

Find the notebook that you want to move to a stack, and tap and hold your finger on the screen. A menu pops up. You can also get this menu to appear with a single tap on the three vertical dots to the right of the notebook name. Here is the menu:

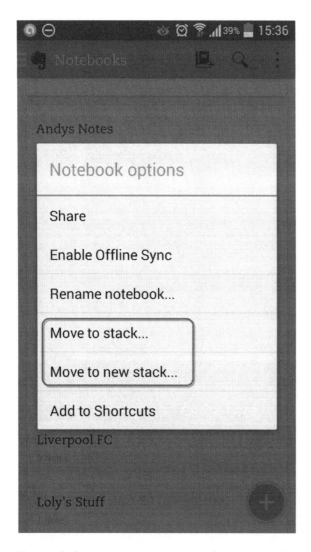

Two of those menu items refer to stacks. **Move to Stack** will show you a list of current stacks, and you tap the one you want to move the notebook into.

If you want to move the notebook into a new stack, tap **Move to new stack** and you'll be prompted for a name for the new stack, which will then be created and your notebook added.

To remove a notebook from a stack, in the Notebooks view, click on the stack to open it up (if necessary), so you can see the individual notebooks in that stack.

Now tap and hold the one you want to move, or click the 3 vertical dots to the right of the name.

A menu opens, with options to **Remove from stack**, **Move to stack** or **Move to new stack**.

iOS
Open the sidebar and tap **Notebooks**.

Click on the **Edit** button top right.

All of the notebooks will have the delete button in front of them, and the **Share** and **Info** buttons at the end. Click the Info button:

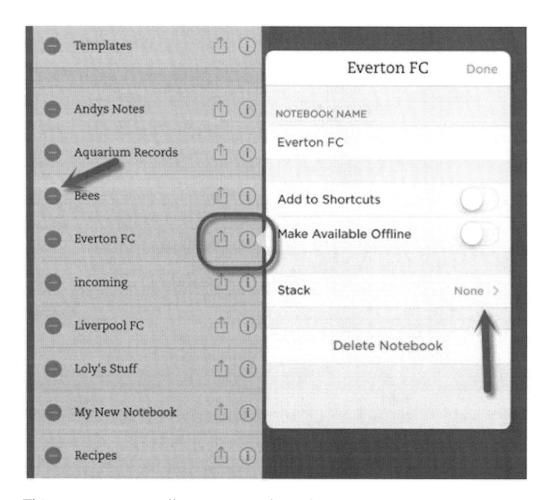

This opens out a smaller screen to the right.

On this screen, you can see an entry called **Stack**, which is currently set to **None >**. Click the **None** link and you'll be presented with a list of currently available stacks. Tap one to add your notebook. If you want to create a new stack, that screen also gives you the option of creating a new stack, simply by entering a name for the new stack.

When you've made your selection (or typed the name of the new stack), click the **Done** button top right.

To remove a notebook from a stack, open the Notebooks screen and find the stack. Expand the stack if necessary so you can see all notebooks in the stack, then click the **Edit** button top right.

Tap on the **Info** icon next to the notebook you want to remove from the stack.

You now have the option to remove the notebook from the stack.

If you simply want to move the notebook to a different stack, tap on the current stack (Liverpool in my screenshot above), and select the new stack from a list (or again, type in the name of a new stack you want to move it to).

How to share entire Notebooks

Evernote allows you to share complete notebooks, either with specific people, or by making the notebook public.

In Evernote Web, move your mouse over the notebook you wish to share. When you do, you'll see a small arrow appear at the right end of the notebook name:

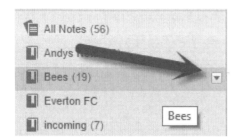

Either click on this, or right click the notebook to open the menu.

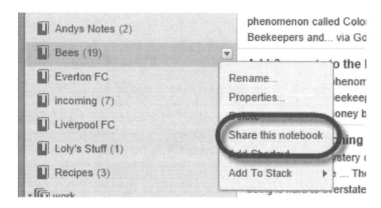

Choose **Share this notebook** from the menu.

You'll now have two options for sharing.

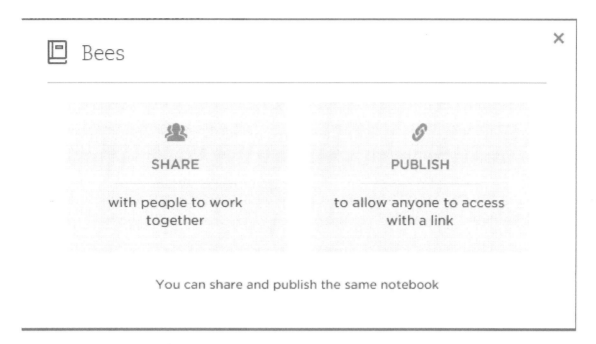

Firstly you can **Share** with specific people. Secondly you can **Publish** the notebook so anyone can access it if they have the link.

Let's share with a specific person:

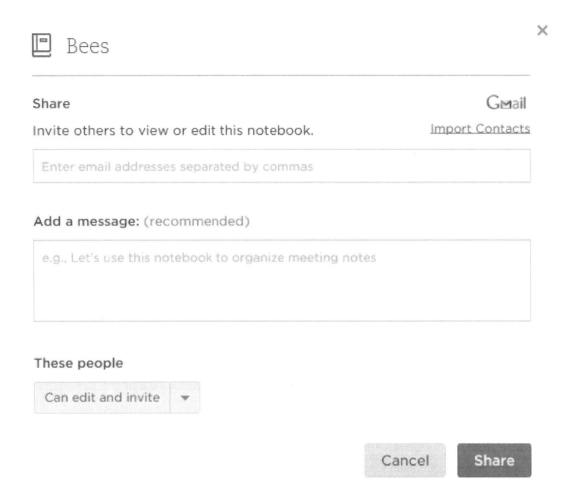

In the email address box, enter the email address(es) of the person(s) you want to share the notebook with. Separate multiple email addresses with a comma.

If the person has an Evernote account already, use their login email address, since they'll be importing the notebook into their own Evernote account. If they don't already have an Evernote account, just use their usual email address and they'll be prompted to create an Evernote account.

Now add a message telling these people what the invitation is about.

In the bottom left, you can choose one of three options. Allow these people to view only, or be able to edit as well, and the final option is to be able to edit and invite other people to share the notebook.

When you've filled this form, the recipients will get an email with a link to click like this:

When they click the Add notebook button, they'll be taken to their Evernote account, where the notebook will be listed in a **Joined Notebooks** section:

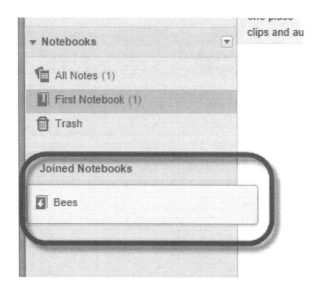

In the screenshot above, you can see this demo account has joined my Bees notebook.

Clicking the link to a joined notebook will open a new tab in your browser, which opens the notebook.

Any changes made to the notebook (by anyone with edit privileges) will be propagated to all users that have joined the notebook.

Shared notebooks like this are great collaborative tools.

At any time, the person that initially shared the notebook has the right to withdraw or modify the sharing rules.

If you mouse over the notebook again and open the menu, you now see a slightly different menu item:

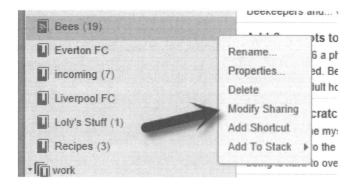

Modify Sharing will open a new screen where you can review who is sharing the notebook, and change or delete their privileges:

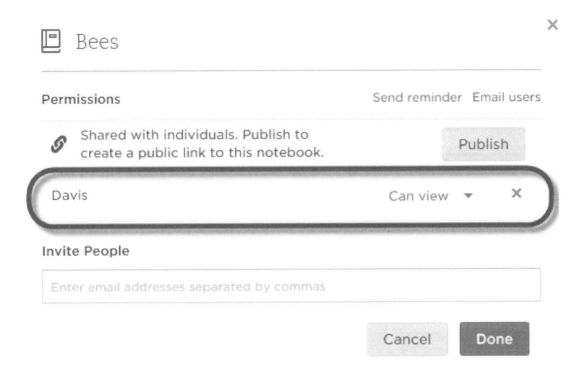

The cross at the end of the line can be used to stop notebook sharing with that person.

The other type of sharing is to publish your notebook so that anyone can access it.

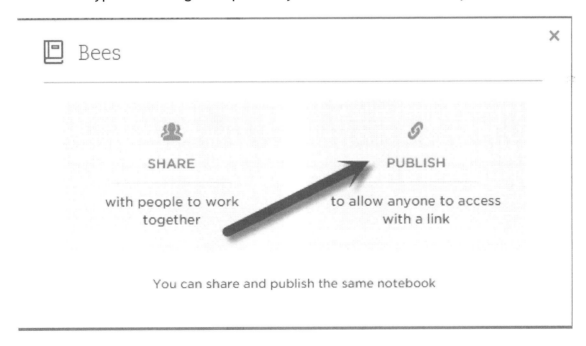

Clicking this button will open this screen:

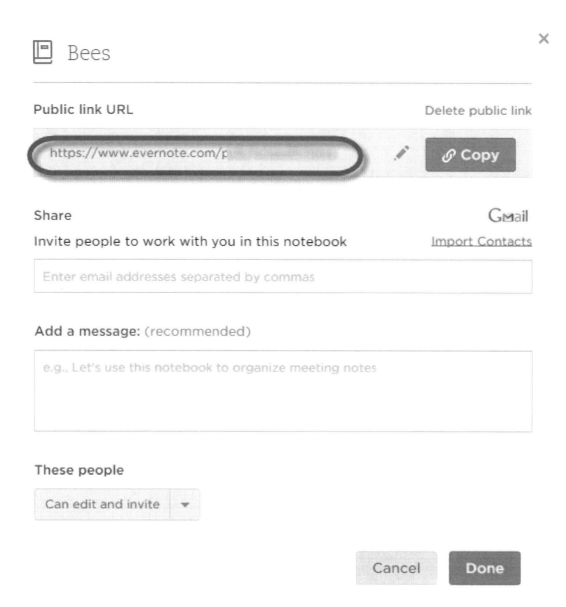

At the top, you can see the public URL that you can share with anyone. You also have the option on this screen to invite people to work with you on the notebook (with view, edit and invite privileges).

OK, that's how to share notebooks using the Evernote Web App, let's see how it can be done on the various devices, starting with the PC.

PC
In the PC version of Evernote, right-click the notebook you want to share to bring up this menu:

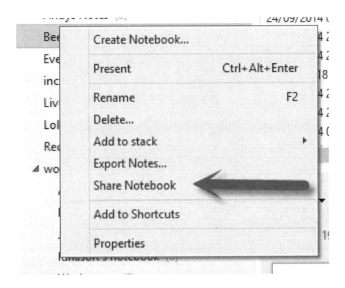

There is a Share Notebook menu item. Click that to start the sharing process. A new screen opens, which is very similar to the one we saw for the Evernote Web app.

Bees

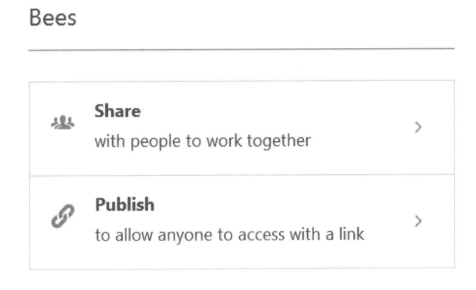

You can share and publish the same notebook

The top option allows you to share with specific people, using their Evernote account email addresses. As seen previously, people you share a notebook with can have edit, read only and invite privileges.

The second option it to create a public notebook, which is essentially a URL you can share with anyone and everyone.

If you have already shared a notebook, and you click on the share notebook menu item, a new screen opens up, with the sharing options:

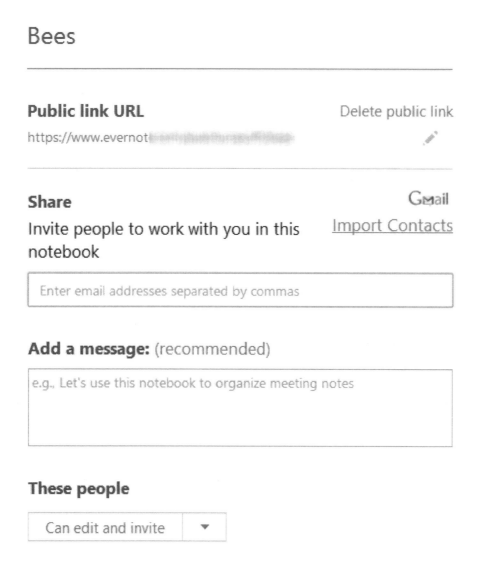

At the top is a URL to make the notebook public. If you've decided that you don't want the notebook public, click the **Delete public link** link. Alternatively you can make the link a little more cryptic by clicking the "edit" pencil, and entering a different name for the shared file.

Mac
To share a notebook in the Mac version of Evernote, right click on the notebook name. This can be in the left sidebar if you have individual notebooks visible, or in the list of notebooks after clicking on the **Notebooks** item in the left sidebar.

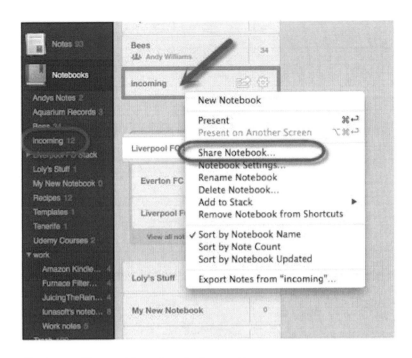

Click on **Share Notebook** from the menu.

A screen opens that allows you to **Share** via email, or **Publish** the notebook. This second option essentially provides you with a URL you can give people:

Click the **Share** option and you'll be invited to enter the email addresses of those you want to share the notebook with. These email addresses should be the email address they use to login to Evernote.

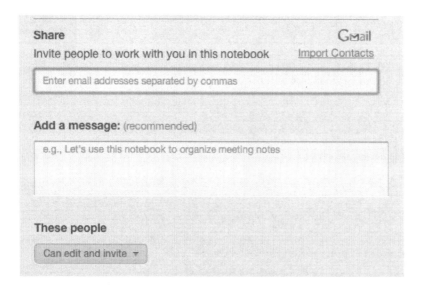

You can invite multiple people by separating their email addresses with a comma, and even enter a small message telling them why you are sending them your notebook.

You also can specify what these people can do with the notebook. Can they edit it, and invite others, or just read it?

If you choose the **Publish** option, Evernote will show you a **Public link URL** that you can give to people.

Note that Evernote shows you the Share option on this screen as well.

NOTE: If you have a shared notebook, and you right click on it in the notebook list, there is no **Share Notebook** menu item. Instead you have a **Modify Sharing** as an option. On this screen you can change the sharing that you set up earlier, removing people's rights or sharing with more people.

Android

Bring up the list of notebooks by opening the sidebar and tapping on **Notebooks**.

Find the notebook you want to share, and long tap and hold, or tap the three vertical dots to the right of the notebook name.

You'll see this menu.

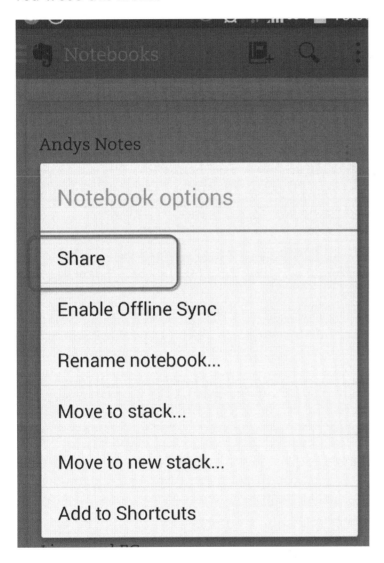

Tap **Share**.

You'll be given an email form to enter the email address of the person you want to share the notebook with. Enter the email address they use to login to their Evernote account.

You'll also be able to specify what they can do with the notebook (read only, or edit / invite others).

iOS

To share a notebook on the iPad, open the sidebar and tap on **Notebooks**. Find the notebook you want to share.

Now tap on the **Edit** link, top right.

After each notebook name, you'll see the **Share** icon and the **Info** icon.

Tap the **Share** icon next to the notebook you want to share.

You'll be given a form to fill in the email address of the person you want to share the notebook with (use their Evernote login email address).

You can also include a short message and specify what that person can do with the notebook (view, edit or edit and invite others).

After entering the details, click the **Share** button top right of that screen.

Working With Notes

How to share your Notes

We saw previously how we can share notebooks with other people. However, you might only want to share a single note.

There are a number of ways you can share your notes with other people.

Within the Evernote Web application (login at Evernote.com), view any note and you'll find a share button in the toolbar above the note.

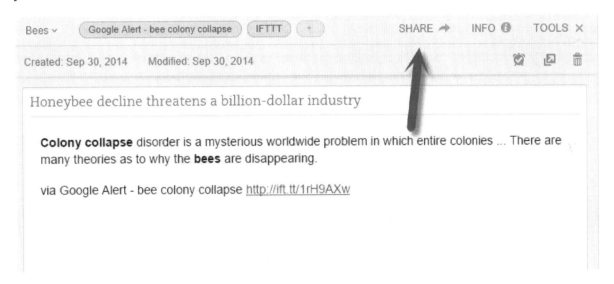

This share button will allow you to share the note via:

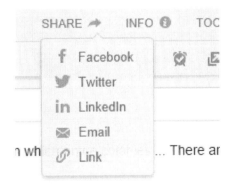

If you choose to share via Facebook, Twitter or LinkedIn, you'll be redirected to authorize Evernote to post to your social channel. Once Evernote has been authorized, the note will be posted to that account.

If you choose to share via email, an email form pops up, and you fill in the recipient email and a short message to accompany your note.

This, together with the note will then be emailed to that address. Here is this message in my own inbox:

The subject line in the email is the same as the title of the note. This couldn't be changed when we sent the email from the Web App.

You can see the short message I added when I sent the email, highlighted in the screenshot above.

If you choose to share the note via a link, Evernote creates a link that you can copy and paste into an email or other document for sharing.

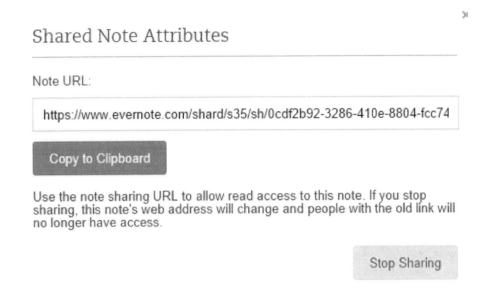

Let's see how to share notes on other platforms.

PC

If you've customized your toolbar, you may have inserted the share button into the toolbar:

If you click the main share button (not the arrow on the right), the default behavior is to share via email. You can choose other sharing options by clicking the arrow next to the word "share". However, since most people reading this probably do not have this share button in their toolbar, let's look at a method everyone does have immediate access to.

When you click on a note and it becomes active, there is a toolbar above the note itself:

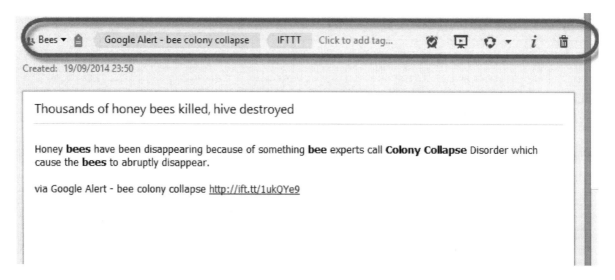

The sharing button looks like three tadpoles swimming in a circle, and has a downward arrow next to it, which opens up the sharing menu:

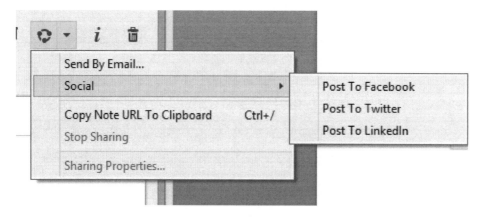

Send by Email is the top option.

The email form this opens is a little more detailed than the one in the Web App.

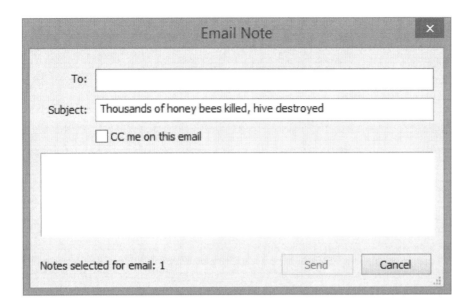

As you can see, below the email address at the top, you also get to enter a subject line for the email. This is pre-filled with the title of the note, but you can edit this if you wish (unlike the Evernote Web App).

You also have the option of sending yourself a copy, by checking the CC box.

Mac

If you have a note you want to share, right click on the note, and select **Share** from the menu:

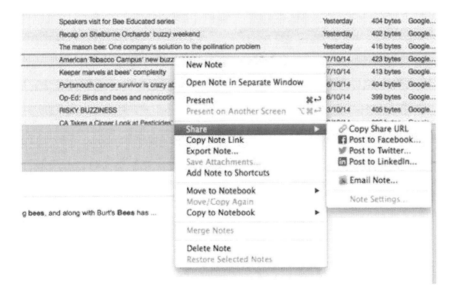

This menu will open out, giving you options to:

- Copy Share URL
- Post to Facebook

137

- Post to Twitter
- Post to LinkIn
- Email Note

If you click on **Copy Share URL**, Evernote will create a publically shareable link and copy it to the clipboard, ready for pasting into whatever document you like. If at some point in the future you want to stop sharing the note, you need to right click the note again and select **Note Settings** (which is disabled in the previous screenshot as this note wasn't already shared), and select the **Stop sharing** option from there.

If you try to post to a social channel, e.g. Facebook, your web browser will open and you'll need to login before Evernote can post to your timeline.

Android
To share a note on Android, open the note and click the menu button top right (three vertical dots). From the menu, select **Share**.

Evernote will offer you the usual **copy URL**, and **Post to Facebook**, but as with any type of sharing on Android devices, you have a lot more options as well (depending on what apps you have installed).

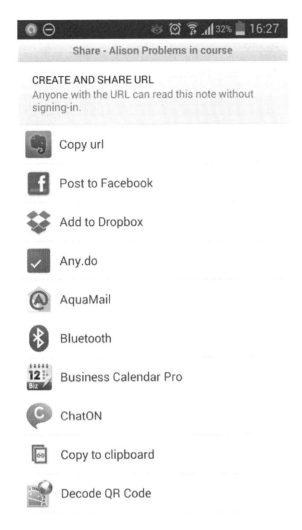

iOS

To share a note on iOS, open it.

Tap on the menu (three horizontal circles, top right), and select **Share**.

You'll get a few options for sharing, so tap the one you want to use:

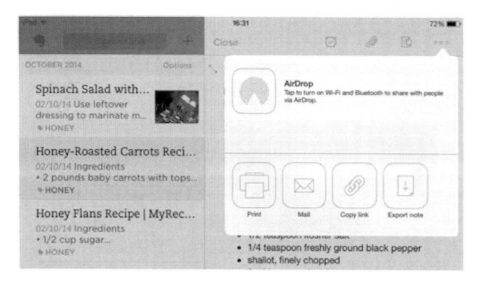

You'll notice you can also print your note from this screen.

How to set reminders in Evernote

One of the advantages of Evernote over, let's say, Sticky notes attached to your monitor, is that you can get Evernote to give you a reminder notification at a pre-arranged date and time.

For example, let's suppose that you have a dental appointment on Monday 6th October at 12:30. You enter this appointment into Evernote, but want Evernote to remind you at 12:00, giving you 30 minutes to get ready and get to your appointment.

OK; here is the note in Evernote:

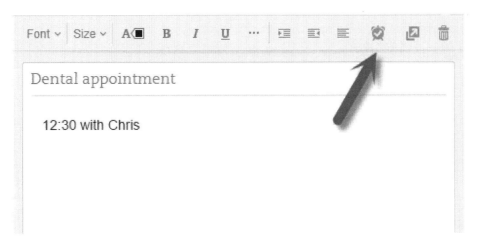

To set the reminder, click on the small alarm clock icon (with the check mark in the middle) and you'll see the message that the reminder was added. However, no time or date has been specified yet.

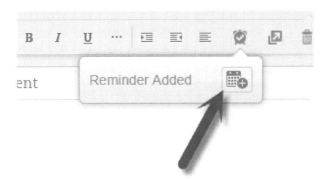

To set the reminder date and time, click the small calendar button.

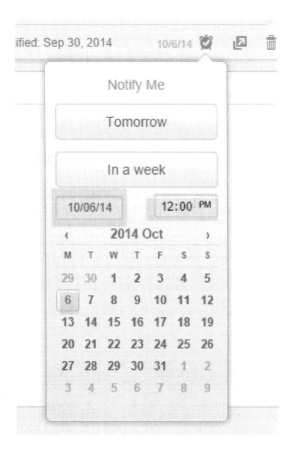

You can now set the date and the time of the reminder.

When 12 pm on the 6th October arrives, Evernote will spring the reminder on you. I find getting these reminders on my android phone, particularly useful.

As an added extra, you can have reminder emails sent to you on the morning the reminder is due. To activate this in Evernote Web, open the Account setting:

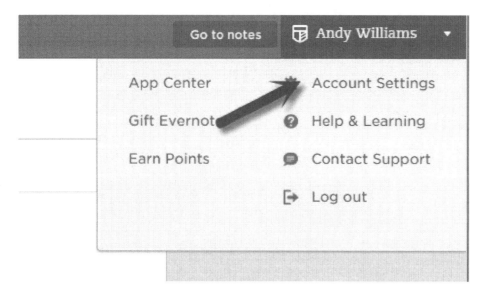

Then click on the **Reminders** tab in the left menu, and finally check the box on this screen:

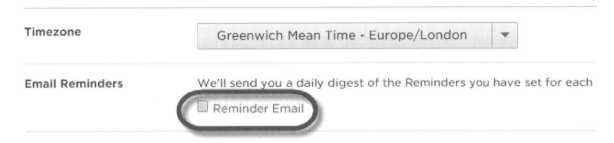

PC

Setting reminders on the PC is very easy. Select the note you want to be reminded about, or create a new one. In the note editing screen, the toolbar right above the note has a button that is identical to the reminder button in the Web Evernote app. It's a small alarm clock with a check mark inside. Click it to make the note into a reminder, and then click the **Add Date** button:

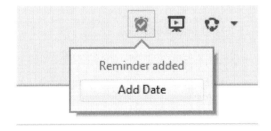

You can then select the date and time:

Once you've made your selection, there is no obvious save button, so just click anywhere on Evernote, away from this popup screen.

You can cancel or change a reminder by clicking the same button again, where you are now given options to **Mark as Done**, **Clear Reminder** and **Change Date**.

To switch on email reminders (which are sent on the morning of the date of the reminder, not at the specific time of the reminder), open the Options screen from the Tools menu.

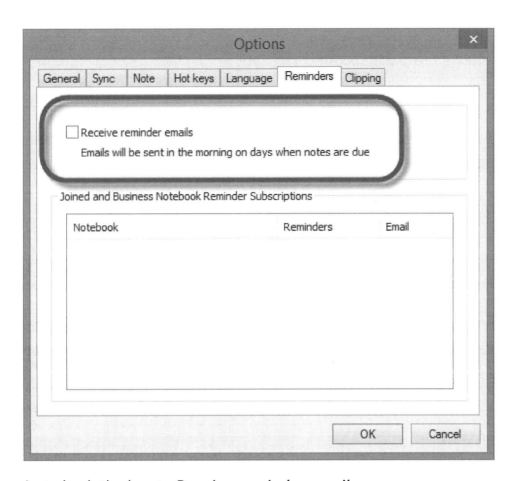

Just check the box to **Receive reminder emails.**

Mac

To set a reminder for a note, click on the alarm clock icon in the note toolbar:

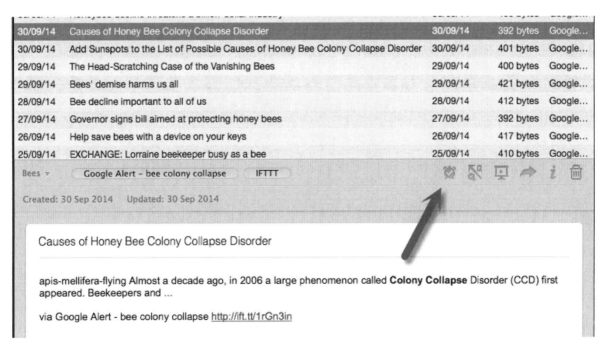

You'll see this icon when you are entering a new note, and also if you open an existing note. Therefore you can go back to older notes and create reminders at any time in the future.

When a reminder is set for a note, the alarm clock icon changes color, so you know a reminder was set, but you'll also get a popup screen:

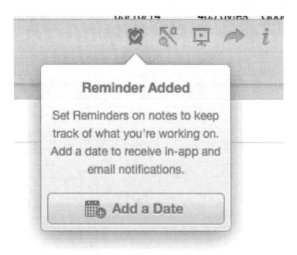

OK, so the reminder was added, but no date or time was set. To set that, click the **Add a Date** button.

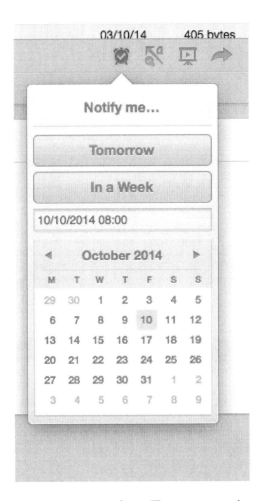

You can now select **Tomorrow**, In **a Week**, or a date from the calendar. Above the calendar, you can see the time, and you can edit that to whatever time you wish the reminder to be triggered on your target date.

If you need to remove a reminder, or change it, you can do so by once again clicking on the alarm button for the note you want to edit:

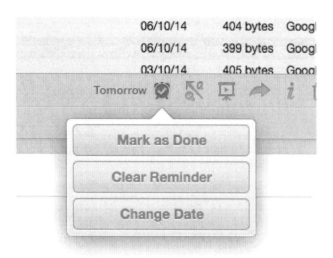

You can now clear the reminder, or change the date/time. Another option here is to mark the reminder as **Done**.

Android

To set a reminder on a note, open the note.

You'll see the alarm clock icon in the note toolbar. Tap it to set a reminder.

When you set the reminder, the date is not set. To set the date, tap on the **Set Date** item in the menu (you see this as soon as you tap the alarm icon).

You'll get a fancy, rather unintuitive screen to set the date:

Try running your finger around that circle. Fun isn't it, even if it is difficult to know which date the reminder is being set for.

OK, an easier way. Leave the circle alone, and tap on **Tomorrow**.

A more familiar date selector will be offered to you. Once you select the date, tap done.

You can also tap the time to open a familiar looking time selector.

When you've set the date and time, click OK and you are done.

The note will now have a colored alarm clock to indicate the reminder has been set. You can change the date / time of the reminder by tapping the alarm clock again.

You'll also be able to tap the alarm clock to mark the reminder as done, or clear the reminder.

iOS

To set the reminder on an iOS device, open the note, and tap on the alarm clock icon in the note toolbar.

A popup screen appears:

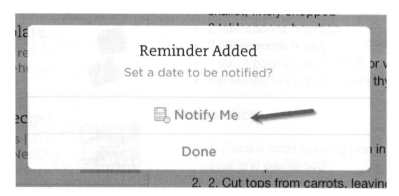

If you don't want to set a date or time for the reminder, click **Done**.

If you want to set a date and time, click the **Notify Me** option.

You will now be given a date/time selector to choose when you want to be notified.

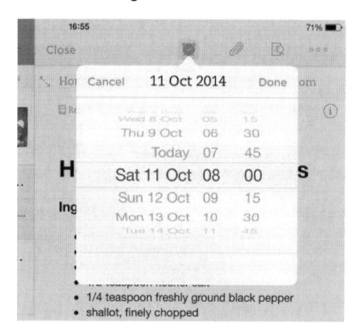

Click **Done** when you have selected the reminder date / time. The alarm clock in the note's toolbar will change color, indicating a reminder has been set.

Tapping the alarm clock again gives you options to mark the reminder as **Done**, **Clear the Reminder**, **Change Date** and **Remove Date**.

Note history

This feature is only available to premium and business users of Evernote, and only on Evernote Web, PC and Mac. It is not available on Android or iOS devices.

Note history allows users to review and restore previous versions of a note. It's useful if you find you've made some mistakes while editing a note, and maybe want to revert back to a version from earlier in the day, or the night before.

To view note history on Evernote Web, open the note, and click the Info button in the note toolbar:

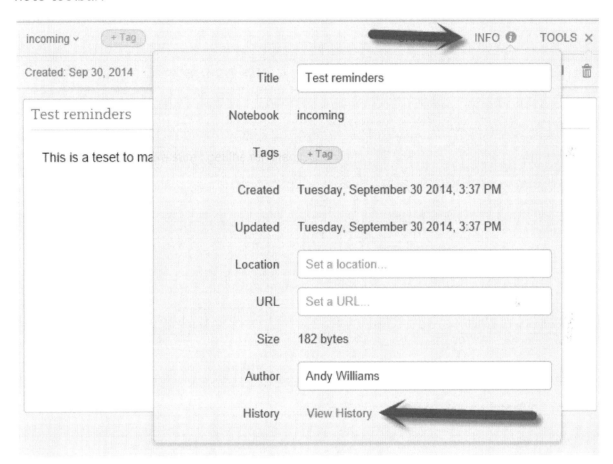

Now you can click the **View History** link.

On the history screen, you'll see a list of the various note versions available. Click a version to view the note. You can copy the contents of a note from this screen and paste it into a new note, or Export the note via this Note History (which will download the note to your computer), then Import it back into Evernote. This process is a lot easier on PC and Mac versions of Evernote.

PC

In the PC version of Evernote, you can access the note history by selecting the note, and clicking the information button in the toolbar.

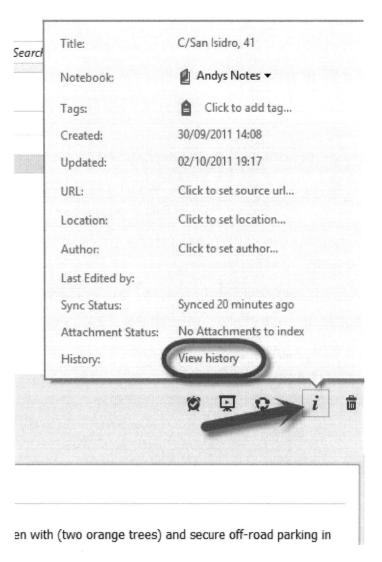

Click on the **View History** link to access the note history for that note.

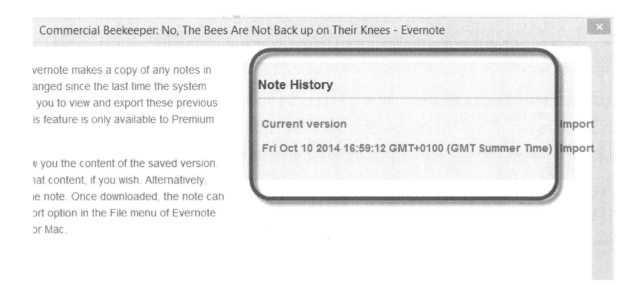

Clicking those versions will open them in a new window, so you can see what they contain. If you find one you'd like to restore, click the Import button. This will actually import the note into a local notebook, but you can move the note to a more appropriate place and delete that local notebook when finished with it.

Mac

On the Mac, you can access the note history by clicking the **Info** icon in the note toolbar.

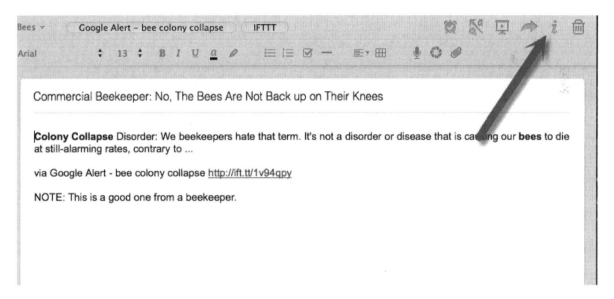

On the Note Information screen, you'll see a link to **View History** at the bottom.

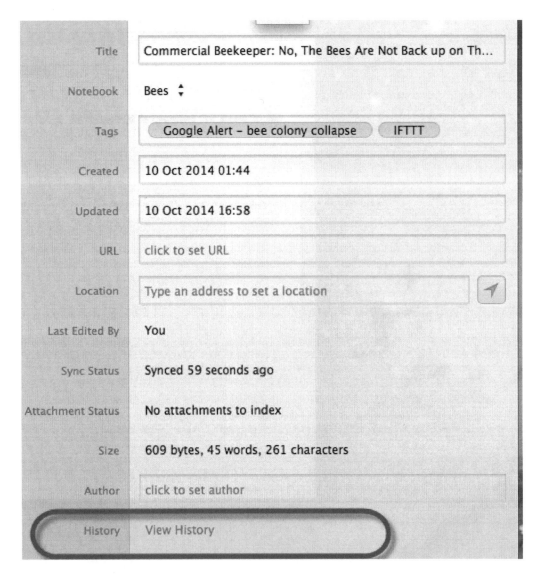

Clicking that link will open a screen that shows the various versions of the note saved by Evernote.

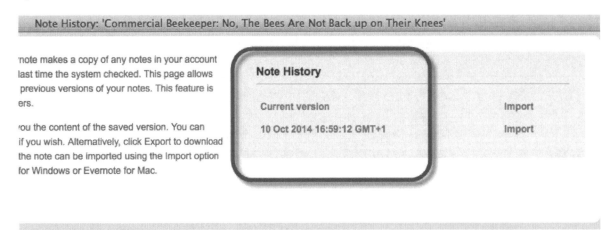

You can click those links to see each version (they open in a new window).

If you find you want to revert back to an older version, you can click the **Import** button. This will actually place the imported note into a local notebook, rather than directly replace the current version of that note in its notebook.

Android
Note History is not available on Android versions of Evernote.

iOS
Note History is not available on iOS versions of Evernote.

How to attach a file in Evernote

You can attach just about any type of file to a note.

- Scanned documents
- Photographs and image
- Sound files
- PDFs
- Spreadsheets and other Office documents

For example, suppose you have a PDF report to read by Monday, and you create a note so you can scribble down your thoughts as you go through the report. Wouldn't it be useful to attach the PDF report to the notes, for quick and easy access?

In the Evernote Web interface, create your note, and then click on the paperclip button. This opens a screen that allows you to attach the PDF to the note:

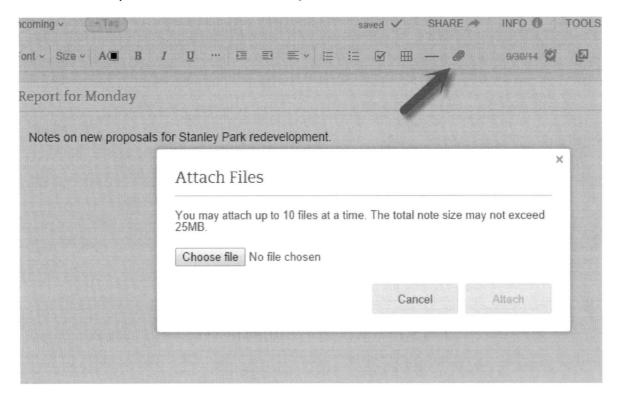

You can use the **Choose file** button to navigate to the PDF on your computer, and select it.

You'll then be given the opportunity to attach more documents to the note. It you're done, click on the **Attach** button.

The PDF will then be uploaded to Evernote servers, making it available on all of your devices.

Your note will show the attachment like this:

To read the report, just click on it to open in your default PDF viewer.

Incidentally, any attachments that are opened and edited in their default program will be updated in Evernote too.

PC

To attach a document in the PC version of Evernote, again, look for the paperclip icon in the note toolbar. If you don't see it, you might see this symbol on the far right:

Click it, as it means there are buttons on your toolbar that are not currently visible.

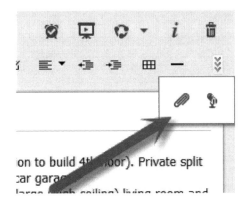

Ahhhh. There is it.

Click the paperclip, and select the PDF you want to attach. The PDF will be added to the note and you'll see the entire PDF within the note body. Hovering your mouse over the PDF reveals PDF navigation buttons.

Stanley Park Note

Need to make notes on this by Monday.

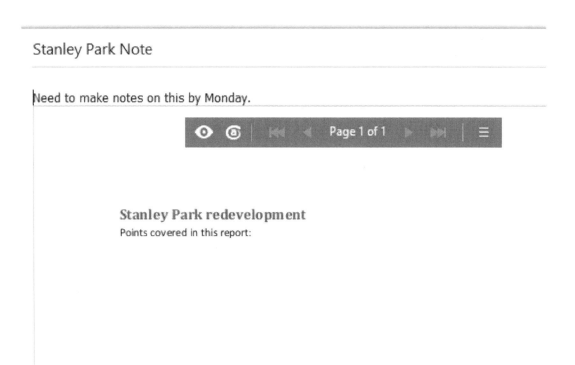

If you double click on the PDF, you can open it in the default PDF viewer on your PC.

Mac
To attach a file on Evernote Mac, open the note and click into the note as if to edit. This makes the toolbar visible.

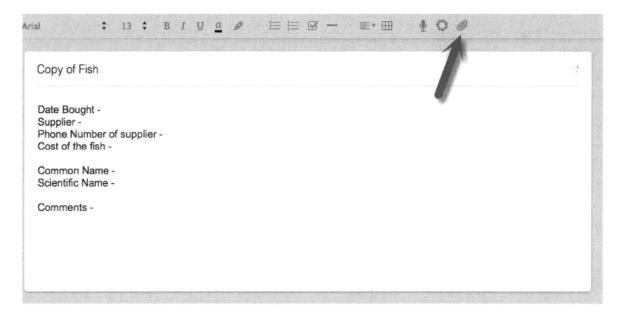

Click on the paperclip icon. You'll get a **Select Files to Attach** dialogue box, so select the files you want to attach.

How Evernote adds the attachment depends on the type of attachment.

I've just selected a single text file in my example:

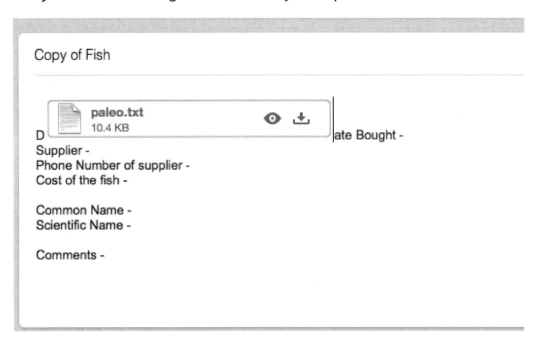

The text file is added as a rectangular attachment box in the body of the note, where the cursor was located before the addition.

This can be clicked, dragged and dropped, to move it anywhere within your note.

This attachment rectangle has two icons. The first is a viewer icon, which opens the attachment in an Evernote internal viewer if possible.

The second icon allows you to save the attachment to your computer.

Play around with attaching different types of files to see how they are handled.

Images should be inserted directly into the note without the attachment rectangle.

PDFs should also be imported in their entirety, though they will have one of these attachment rectangles at the top of the PDF, which allows you to open the PDF in an external PDF viewer.

There are three icons in the attachment rectangle at the top of the PDF. The first one "annotate", opens the PDF in a special PDF viewer / Editor built into Evernote. I'll leave you to try that for yourself.

Sound files will be attached inside an attachment rectangle, but there will be a play button inside the rectangle to play the file directly from within the note.

Android
On Android, you can attach a document by opening the note you want to attach it to.

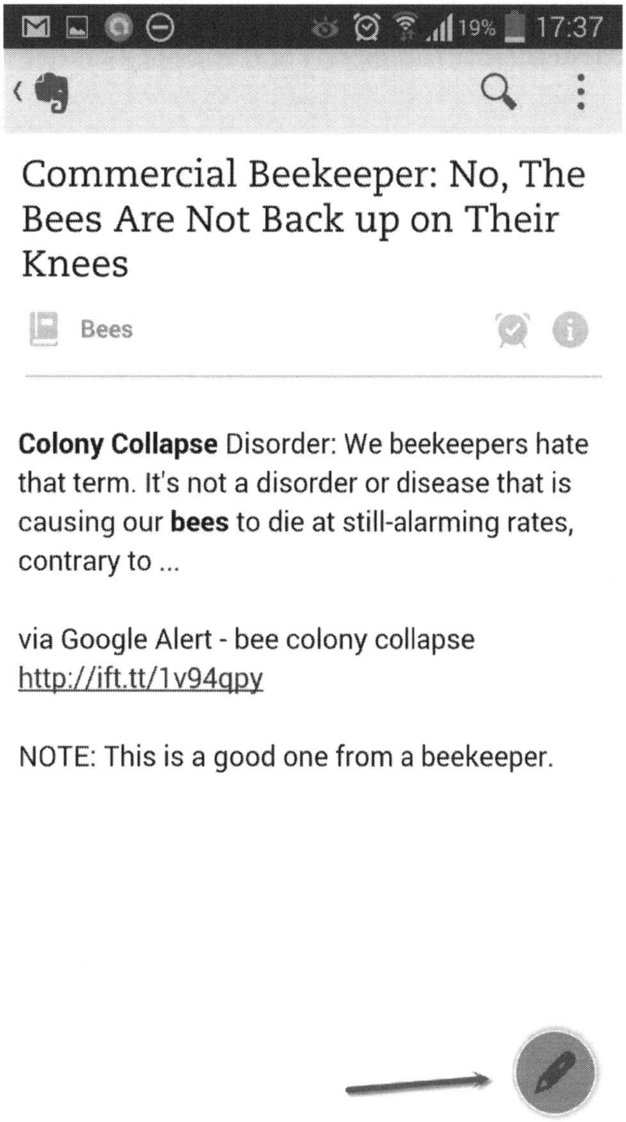

Commercial Beekeeper: No, The Bees Are Not Back up on Their Knees

Bees

Colony Collapse Disorder: We beekeepers hate that term. It's not a disorder or disease that is causing our **bees** to die at still-alarming rates, contrary to ...

via Google Alert - bee colony collapse
http://ift.tt/1v94qpy

NOTE: This is a good one from a beekeeper.

Click on the Edit button bottom right.

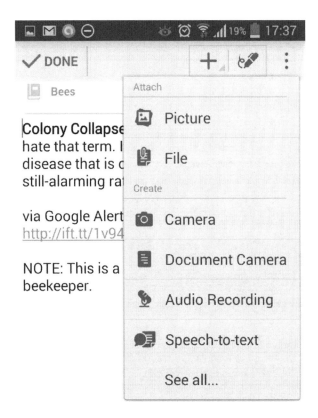

Now click on the "+" button in the toolbar, which opens a menu allowing you to attach a picture or file. If you click the **See all...** link at the bottom, you'll also get options for video and audio.

On this menu, you also have a section called **Create** which allows you to take a photo with your camera to attach to the note. I'll leave you to explore the other possible media formats that can be attached via this screen.

iOS

If you are creating a new note, you can attach photos and audio to the note by clicking the camera or microphone icons in the toolbar. If the note is already saved, you'll need to attach these in a different way.

Open the document you want to attach something to.

In the toolbar at the top, click the paperclip icon and you'll be given options to attach various types of documents, including photos and audio. You also have access to Evernote's **Document Camera** which is there to help you go paperless.

How to delete attachment in Evernote

You'd think that something as easy as deleting an attachment would be fairly intuitive wouldn't you? Well a lot of people struggle with this.

In Evernote Web, to delete an attachment, you can click in the white space to the right of the attachment:

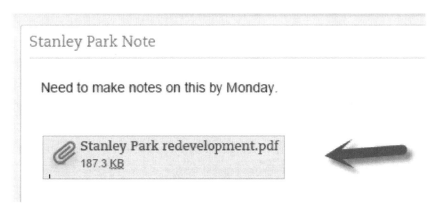

That should move the cursor to the right side of the attachment, or even possibly inside the attachment box to the right of the "KB". Now just press the delete key on your keyboard. If your cursor was outside the attachment box, this should delete the attachment in one go. If your cursor was inside the attachment box you may need to press delete a few times to remove everything. You might even be left with the box without any attachment information inside, like this:

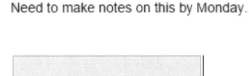

In that case, keep using your delete key to target that pesky box. Eventually you will delete it.

This isn't simple and it's not fun. I do hope that Evernote design an easier way of doing this.

PC

On a PC, it's just as much of a problem to delete attachments, and you do it the same way as the Evernote Web app.

Move your mouse cursor to the right of the attachment box and click, to set your cursor. Now click the delete button.

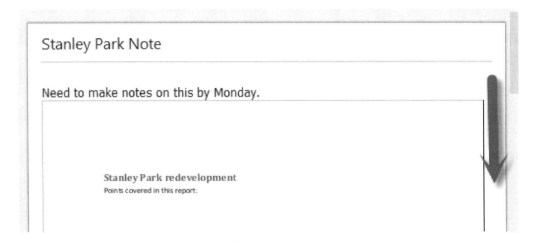

This should delete the attachment.

Mac
To delete an attachment in Evernote Mac, move your mouse cursor to the right hand side of the attachment rectangle and click to set your cursor position. Now press the delete key on your keyboard.

Images can also be deleted in this way.

Android
Attachments in Android come with their own menu button:

this is a test
What is my title

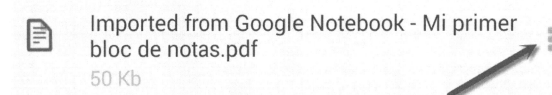

Tap the menu button and select **Delete** to remove the attachment. You can also **View**, **Edit** and **Download** the attachment from this menu.

iOS

On iOS devices, tap to the right of the attachment to set the cursor position:

Done

Must read

This is important to look through before meeting

Tap to Download

Savings.xlsx

14.0 KB

Now tap the delete key on your on-screen keyboard.

How to access Evernote offline

This is a question I see a lot. You're about to travel somewhere and don't think you'll have internet access. How can you make sure your Evernotes are available to you, even without WIFI?

Well, it's a little complicated. Let's consider the free Evernote users first.

First of all, you can access all notes on a PC or Mac computer whether or not you're connected to the internet. The problem arises on mobile devices.

All notes you create in Evernote are stored on Evernote's servers, in the cloud, so they can be synced between all of your devices. However, on mobile devices, all notes are also stored locally in a cache (similar to the way your web browser caches web pages you visit). When you are without an internet connection, the notes in the cache will be available to use. If a note is in the cache, you'll be able to view it. If it is not in the cache, you won't.

While you are offline, you can create new notes, which will be synced to the cloud (and therefore all of your other devices) when your device reconnects to the internet.

To be absolutely sure you can access all notes offline, you need a premium account, which is around $5 per month (5€ a month in Europe).

Premium users can choose to take one or more of their notebooks offline. In doing so, everything in the notebook will be downloaded locally to the device and saved, giving you permanent access to those notebooks offline.

Since taking a notebook offline means you are telling Evernote to download the notebook to your device, you need to enable this feature on the mobile device itself.

Let's see how to do this, starting with an Android device.

Android

Open the sidebar and tap **Notebooks.** Now tap the menu button next to the notebook you want to share:

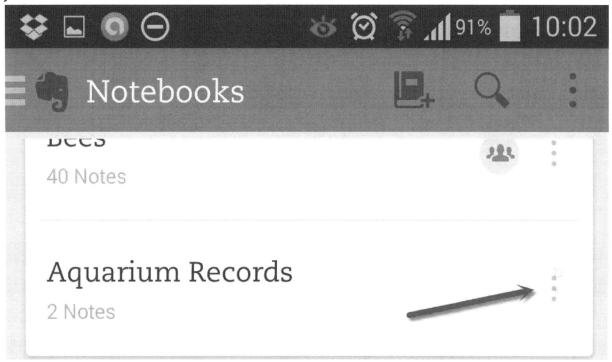

The menu has the following options:

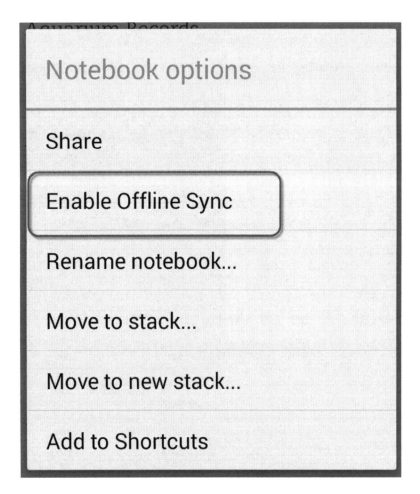

Tap the **Enable Offline Sync** to activate the feature.

iOS
On iOS devices, open the sidebar and tap **Notebooks**.

Now tap the **Edit** button top right.

Next to the notebook you want to set for offline viewing, tap the **Info** icon. A menu opens:

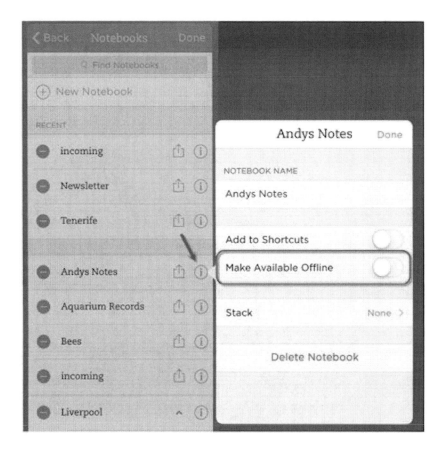

Tap on the **Make Available Offline** button to activate the feature.

How to access Evernote trash & Empty it

You've just accidentally deleted your school homework, and panic strikes. It was due this morning. You start planning your excuse.

"Miss, Evernote ate my homework" has a nice ring to it. The problem is that she'll never believe it.

Why?

She'll just ask why you didn't retrieve it from the trash.

Trash? In Evernote?

Whenever you delete a note in Evernote, it gets sent to the trash. A lot of people have great difficulty finding the trash, especially those using Android devices, because they don't have a trash bin.

To access the trash, you'll need to login to Evernote Web, or use a PC, Mac or iOS device.

In the Evernote Web interface, look in the left sidebar, at the bottom of the Notebooks section.

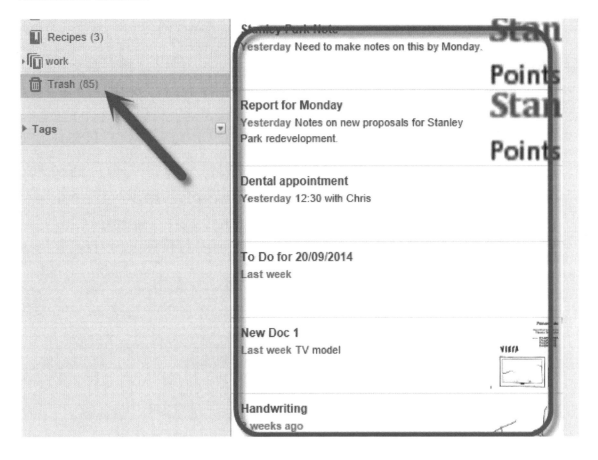

Click on that, and all notes you've deleted will be listed in the notes panel.

Click on the one you want to save, and drag & drop it into a notebook of your choice. The note will be saved to that notebook.

To empty the trash from Evernote Web, mouse over the trash to enable the drop down button at the end, and click that. You can then select **Empty Trash** from the menu that appears.

PC
On the PC version of Evernote, the trash folder is in the same place as the Evernote Web application. Look at the bottom of your list of notebooks in the left sidebar:

Click on the trash folder, and all notes in the trash will be listed. Drag and drop the notes you wish to recover into one of your notebooks.

You can right click on any note in the trash to display this menu:

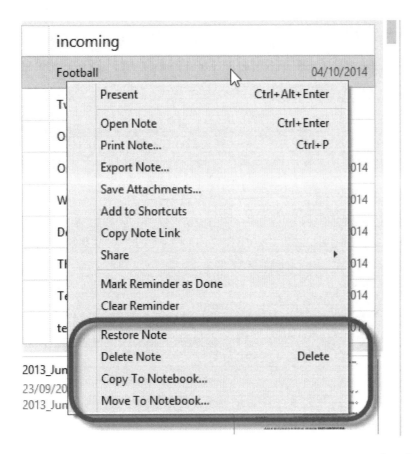

From this, amongst other things, you can restore individual notes, delete them, or move / copy to a notebook.

If you wish to empty the trash, right-click on the Trash item in the sidebar, and select **Empty Trash.**

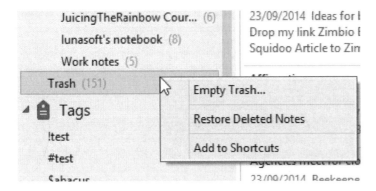

You can also restore deleted notes with this menu.

Mac

The trash folder can be accessed from the left sidebar. It's under the Notebooks:

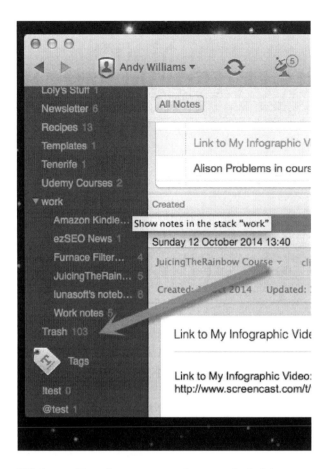

Click on **Trash** to open the trash folder.

You can right click on any note in the trash folder, and get options to restore the note, or delete it permanently.

If you want to empty the trash, you can do so by right-clicking **Trash** in the left sidebar:

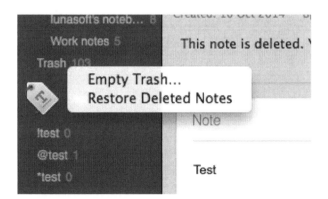

You also have the option of restoring all deleted notes from that menu.

Android

The Android version of Evernote does not have a trash feature. This is probably because mobile devices don't always have spare storage, and trash is stored locally. Since notes can be many MegaBytes in size, the development team probably thought it was best to leave this feature out.

Although there is no trash feature on Android, that does not mean your deleted notes are not recoverable. Deleted notes on Android devices are sent to the trash on the server, so you can recover them, but you'll need the Evernote Web, Desktop versions or an iOS device.

iOS

Unlike the Android version of Evernote which does not have a Trash feature, the iOS version does. It's located at the bottom of the left sidebar.

Clicking on **Trash** will open the trash folder. You can **Empty the Trash** using the link:

If you want to restore any notes, swipe the note from right to left:

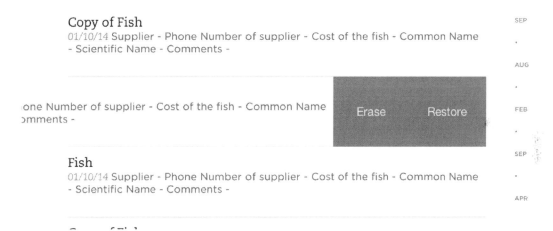

You'll then have the option to **Erase** or **Restore** the note.

How to sort Evernote alphabetical

You can sort your notes in a number of different ways. Alphabetical, by date, recently updated, etc.

Let's look at how to access the sort features, and use alphabetical sort order as an example.

We'll start with the Evernote Web application.

Select the notebook you want to sort or even click on the All Notes at the top.

At the bottom of the list of notes, you'll see a button, linked to a menu, with the label **View Options**. Click it to open the **Sort By** menu:

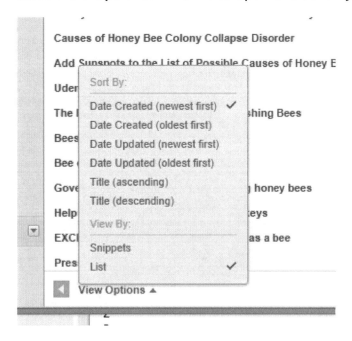

From this menu, you can sort by date created (newest or oldest first), date updated (newest or oldest first), and by title, which sorts alphabetically. Title (ascending) will sort notes from A to Z, while title (descending) will sort notes from Z to A.

Whatever you choose for your sort order is remembered between sessions, so if you log out, then log back in later, your chosen sort order is retained.

Let's see how to sort on the various devices.

PC
On the PC version of Evernote, select a notebook.

If you have your notes shown in **List view**, you can order the notes simply by clicking in the column headers.

Click once to organize to organize "high to low", and again to reverse the order from "low to high".

You can order your notes by any of the column headers this way.

You also have another option for ordering your notes, which you'll have to use anyway if your notes are shown in snippet or card view. It's this small button shown in all three views:

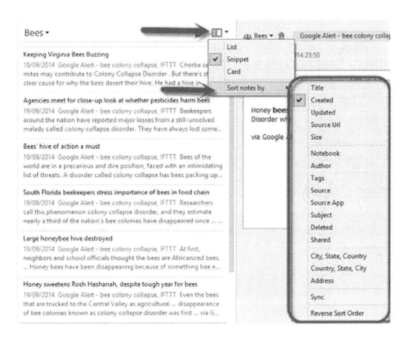

Clicking the button opens a menu with **Sort notes by** being the bottom item. Moving your mouse over **Sort notes by** opens a sub-menu with all of the options shown above.

The top item is to sort by title, which will put the notes in alphabetical order from A to Z. If you want notes from Z to A, you need to click the bottom option of this menu to **Reverse Sort Order.**

Mac

If you are using the **Side List View** or **Top List View** with Evernote Mac, you can order your notes by clicking directly into the column header (these are not visible in the other views). So, clicking on **Title** will order the notes alphabetically, toggling between A to Z and Z to A.

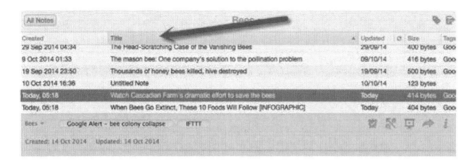

Similarly you can click on the other column headers to order by date, size, etc.

Another way of ordering your notes is to use the **View Options** menu.

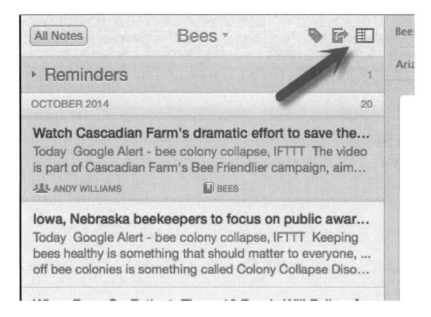

This button changes its appearance to represent the "view" you are currently using to display your notes. Click the button to open the **View Options** menu and move your mouse down to the last row – **Sort by: ...**

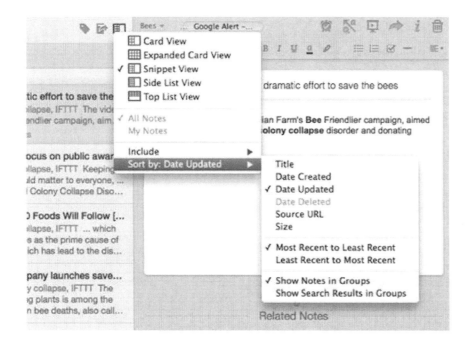

You have options to sort by date, title (alphabetical), source URL and size.

Within your sort choice, you can choose to have notes sorted from most recent to least recent or vice versa. E.g. if you sort by date created, then all notes created on the same day will be sorted using your selection (most recent first is the default).

You can also choose to display your notes in groups. The grouping depends on the way you are sorting your notes. E.g. if you sort alphabetically, then all notes beginning with an "A" will appear in the same group, all notes beginning with "B" another, and so on. If you sort by date, all notes created on the same date will appear in the same group:

Be aware that the **Show Notes in Groups** is not available in all views (e.g. Side and Top view).

Android

On Android devices, click the menu button top right:

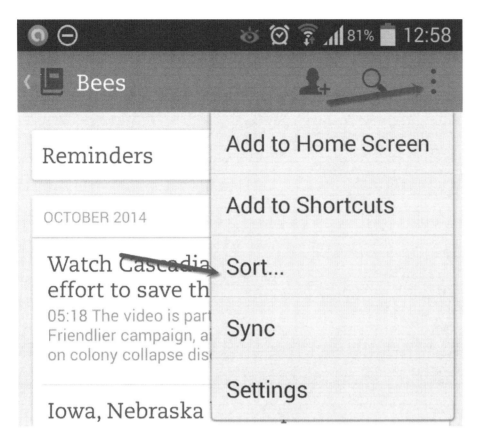

Then click on **Sort...**

This opens a popup screen that gives you the sorting options:

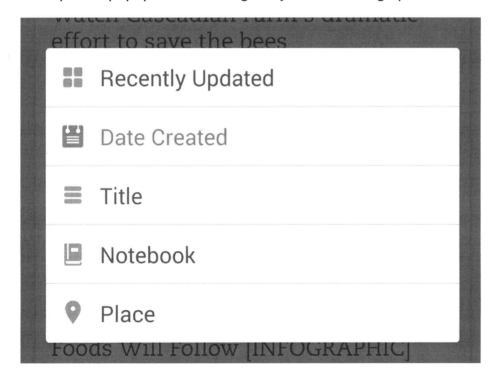

You can sort alphabetically by tapping on **Title**. You can also sort by when the notes were updated, or created.

The 4th option on this list is **Notebook**. This will display all notes into their respective notebooks:

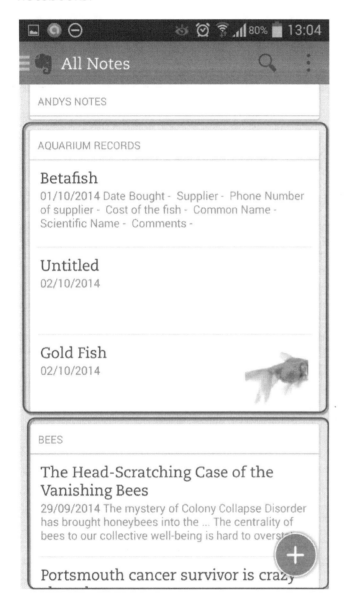

Sorting by Place will create groups of notes created at the same location:

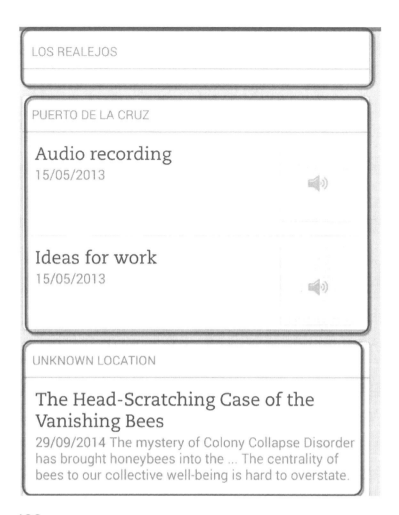

iOS

You can sort any list of notes. For example, you can open a notebook and sort those notes, or carry out a search query and sort the results.

At the top right of a list of notes is an **Options** link. Tap it.

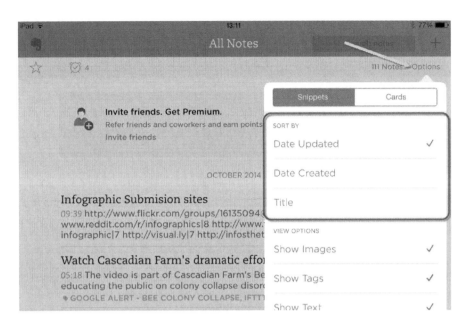

This opens the **View** menu, allowing you to sort by date updated, date created, or alphabetically by title.

If you sort alphabetically by title, you'll see the alphabet down the right side of your screen, where you can tap a letter to jump to notes beginning with that letter:

How to print Evernote notes

Previous versions of Evernote had a print button for quick and easy printing of notes. The latest version seems to have removed that button, but there is a way to add it back (at least on a PC), and another way of printing a note even without the button.

Let's start with the Evernote Web.

The first option for printing is to right click the note you want to print (works in list or snippet view) from the list, and select **print** from the popup menu:

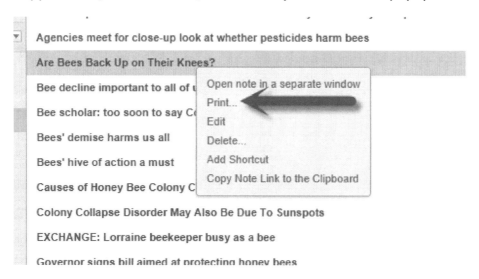

The second option is to right click on the open note, and select print from that menu:

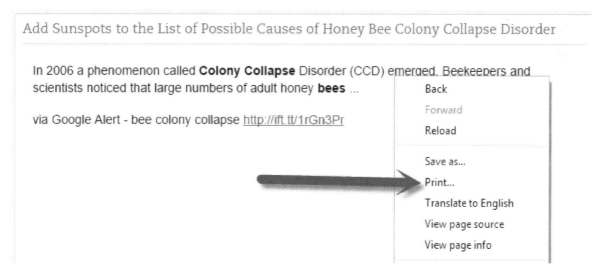

Let's see how to do this on other devices, starting with the PC version of Evernote.

PC

The first option you have on a PC is to add the print button back to you toolbar. Check out the earlier "how to" on customizing the toolbar. Clicking that button will print the currently selected note(s).

The other way of printing notes on the PC Evernote is to right click the note in the note list (this won't work on the note preview panel), and selecting **print** from the menu.

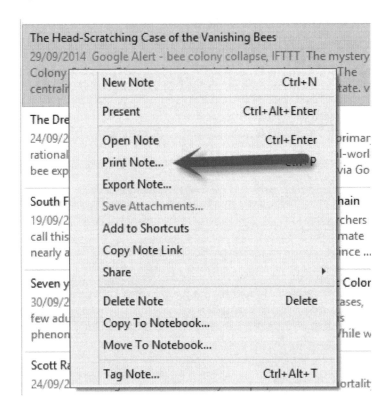

If you want to print more than one note, select them from the list using CTRL+click. As you select more, they become highlighted in your note list. In the main note preview panel, you'll see that change too, now highlighting all of the notes you've selected.

This screen gives you a few different options, but what we want to do is print, so click that print button in your toolbar, or choose **Print** from the **File** menu.

Mac

On the Mac, you can print any note that is currently open by pressing Command + P.

Alternatively, you can access the print feature from the **File** menu at the top.

If you want to print multiple notes, you can select several of them using the Command + Click repeatedly to highlight all the notes. As they are selected, you'll see a visual representation of the selected notes:

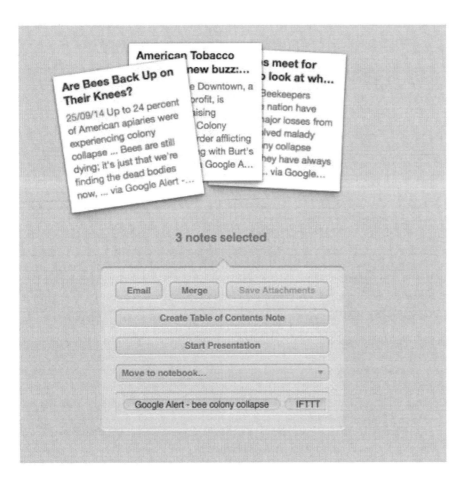

You can then print these notes using the Command + P or the **Print Notes** option from the **File** menu.

Android
Whether you can print or not from your Android will depend on what apps you have installed on your device.

Open the note you want to print, and click the menu button (three vertical dots) top right. Now tap on **Share**, and see what options are available.

If you need to be able to print from your mobile, check out the **PrinterShare Mobile Print** app for Android.

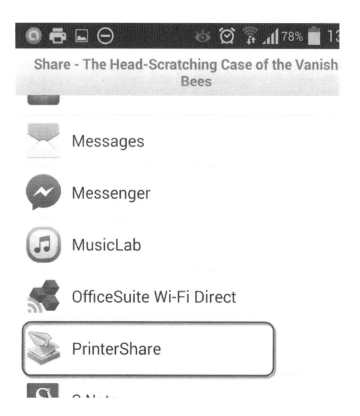

Once you install the app, you need to set your printer up, but then you should be able to print from any app on your device that supports sharing documents.

iOS

To print from an iOS device, open the note you want to print.

Tap the menu button top right (three horizontal dots) and select **Share** from the menu:

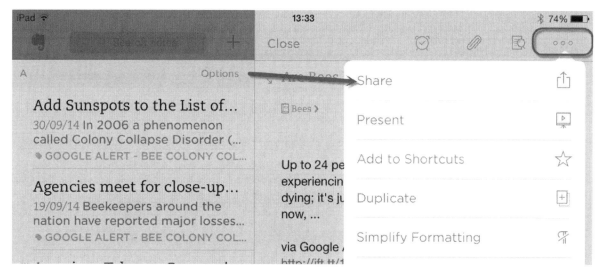

You'll have options to **Print** from that menu.

How to use Evernote handwriting recognition /Image OCR

A lot of people ask about Evernote OCR (optical character recognition), which is the same as handwriting recognition. I should also say something up front. Evernote will search for text within hand-written notes (to display those notes in search results), but Evernote cannot extract that text from hand-written notes and convert them into digital typed notes. Hand-written notes will always be hand-written notes.

OK, let's look at this feature and why it is useful.

Imagine you have a paper notebook with page after page of handwritten notes. It's impossible to search through those notes in an automated way to find a specific section.

Evernote has handwriting recognition built in now, which means when you search for stuff, your hand-written notes will also be searched. Evernote tries to decipher your scribblings to determine what words are there.

It's not perfect, and the worse your writing, the less chance Evernote has of working out what you wrote. However, if your handwriting is fairly neat, you'll find Evernote can easily find words inside handwritten notes.

Let me show you an example.

I created a handwritten note on my Smartphone to remind me about an appointment I had with my son's teacher at school. At the time, I forgot to set a reminder for the note, so I now want to set one. The problem is I cannot find the note.

I know that I mentioned the word "teacher" in the note that I wrote, so if I search for that in Evernote (I'm searching here in the PC version), this is what I get:

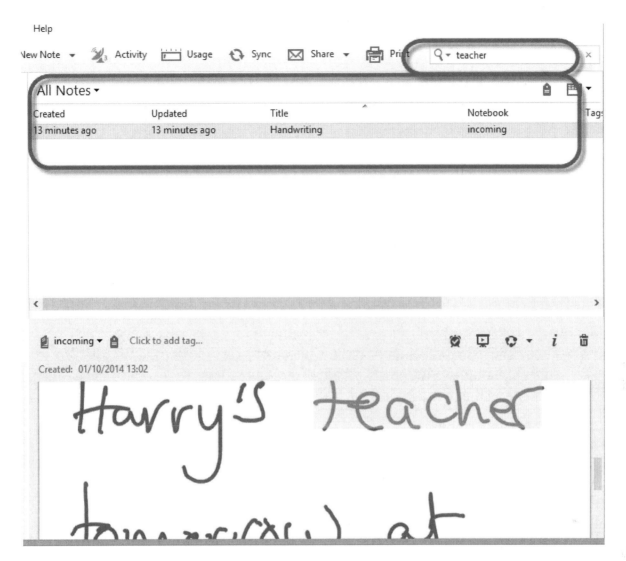

You can see my search phrase at the top is "teacher". Evernote lists all notes that match that phrase, in this case only one. In the note preview window, I can see my handwritten note, with the word teacher highlighted by Evernote.

I can open the note to see the full handwritten note, or simply click on the alarm/reminder button to set a reminder for that note.

Play around with it to see how well it works for your own hand writing. I find that I have to be extra careful when writing if I know I'll want to be able to search for words in the note later on.

How to spell check in Evernote

If you are working in Evernote Web, the spell checking ability of Evernote depends on the browser you are working in. Most include built in spell checkers, so typing an incorrect word will cause a squiggle to appear underneath the word in question, like this:

cial proof from variety of sources you get backlinks from:
Backlinks - good source of content - USAs
   • article marketing done propery
   • forum participation
   • youtube & other video sites
   • RSS feeds
   • Twitter
   • Facebook page

Right clicking the misspelled word opens a menu that gives you suggestions, allows you to add the word to the dictionary, and a lot of other options, all based on your browser and applications you have installed on your computer. I am using Google Chrome, and this is the menu I get:

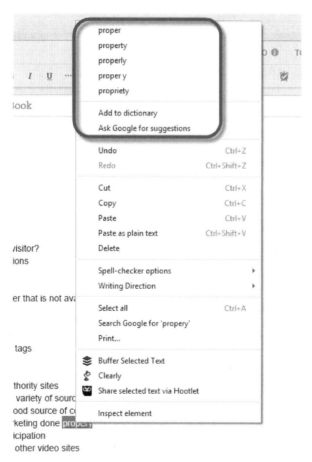

194

You can just click the correct spelling offered, and your document will be updated.

Mobile versions of Evernote do not include spell checking, though your device should check spelling as you type, giving you the opportunity to correct spelling as you go.

Desktop versions of Evernote do have their own spell checking features, so if you ever need to carry out a full spell check on something, sync your notes and open on your desktop computer. Let's look at spell checking on those.

PC

On the PC version of Evernote, to spell check a note, press F7.

If you like using menus, you can find the **Check Spelling** option at the bottom of the **Edit** menu:

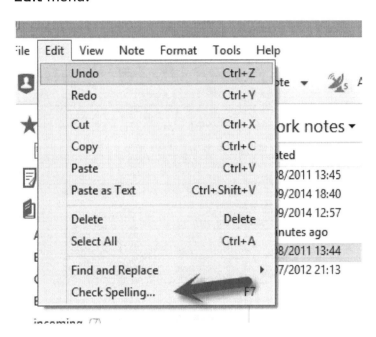

Clicking the **Check Spelling** (or pressing F7) will open the spell check screen:

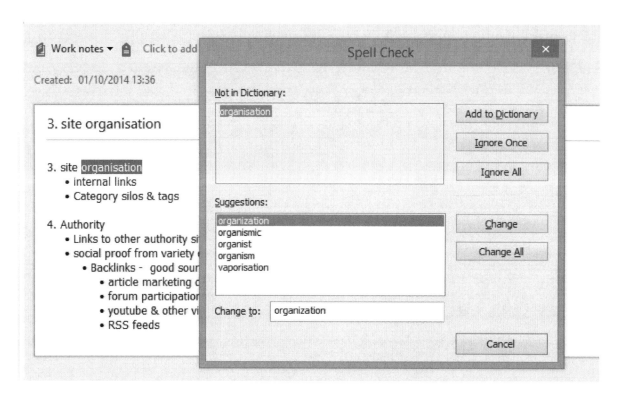

This will go through the note, highlighting any words it does not recognize. It will offer suggestions and give you the opportunity to add the word to the dictionary, if you know it is correct.

To choose one of the suggestions to replace your misspelled word, simply double click the correct word, or single click it and then click the **Change** button.

Mac

Evernote for Mac can check spelling and grammar as you type. Inside the **Edit** menu, there are a few options related to spelling and grammar.

You can select **Show Spelling and Grammar** to start a check on your note. This will go through the entire note, offering you options when problems are found.

The **Check Spelling** option will start the spell check on the note, where unknown words are highlighted sequentially. Press Command + ; to scroll through all misspelled words.

I'm not sure if it is a bug in the version I am running, but there is no check mark next to the **Check Spelling While Typing** option to indicate it is selected. However, this option is clearly enabled as misspelled words get a squiggly line underneath. If I click the **Check Spelling While Typing** option, there is no visual change to the menu item, yet the spelling while typing is disabled as I stop getting the squiggle when I mistype words.

When you read this, Evernote may have fixed this, but if you are having trouble understanding why spelling is not working, try clicking the **Check Spelling While Typing** option.

Once this feature is activated, any misspelled words are underlined with a squiggle. You can right-click or CTRL+Click these words to bring up options:

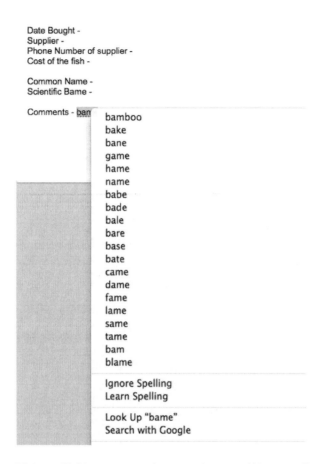

Date Bought -
Supplier -
Phone Number of supplier -
Cost of the fish -

Common Name -
Scientific Bame -

Comments - bam

This will list some alternative spellings, allow you to ignore the spelling, or **Learn Spelling** which adds it to your dictionary.

How to change the Spell Check Dictionary

I live in Spain, but my preferred language is English. Most computer programs assume that because I live in Spain, I want to work in Spanish. I don't.

Fortunately, Evernote gives you options to change the language of the Evernote interface AND the spell checking language.

Since the spell checker in the Evernote Web app is dependent on the browser you are using and not Evernote itself, you cannot change the spell checking language in Evernote Web, you'd need to change the language your browser is using for spell checking. However, Evernote Web does have a couple of language settings.

In Evernote Web, go to the **Account Settings** screen.

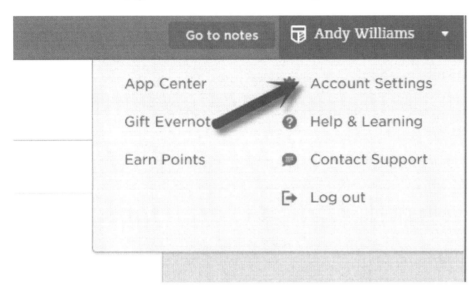

In the left sidebar, select **Personal Settings**.

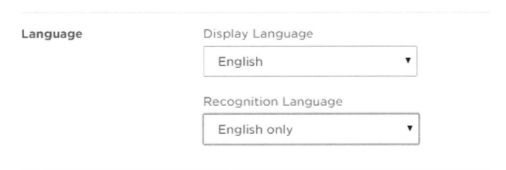

You now have the option of setting your display language (the one used by the Evernote interface), and the recognition language (the one used for handwriting/image recognition).

Let's see what options are available on the PC and Mac versions.

PC

The spell checking and language options in Evernote for PC are found in the **Options** screen under the **Tools** menu.

Click on the **Language** tab:

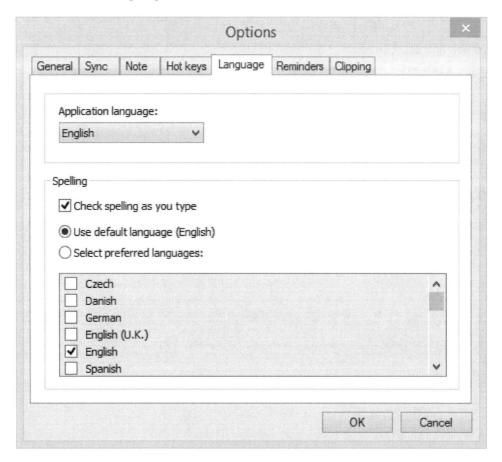

The top drop down box allows you to change the language used in the Evernote user interface. This will be the language used in the menus and messages that Evernote displays.

Under that, you have the spelling options. You can check the box shown to have Evernote spell check as you type. Misspelled words will be marked with a squiggle, giving you the opportunity to correct them with a right click.

The other option is the actual language of the dictionary. By default, the same language that you chose for application language will be selected, but if you want to choose a different language, you can select the **Select preferred languages** radio button, and then check one or more boxes. This is useful if you want to be able to write notes in more than one language. For example, most of my notes are in English, but I might have some in Spanish. I don't want my Spanish notes to be full of squiggles (as Evernote won't recognize them as English words), so checking Spanish as well as English means words from both languages are accepted.

Mac
On the Mac, the language used for spelling is dependent on the settings of your Mac

Launch **System Preferences**.

Click on **Keyboard**.

Click on the **Text** tab.

Under **Spelling**, choose your language from the drop down box:

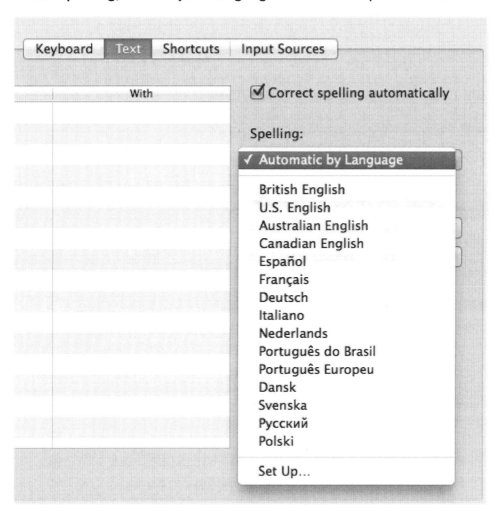

The default is **Automatic by Language**, and this is probably the best setting for most people.

Note encryption

It is possible to encrypt the contents of a note. It is not possible to encrypt entire notebooks.

PC

Highlight the text you want to encrypt, and right click on it. From the menu, select **Encrypt Selected Text**:

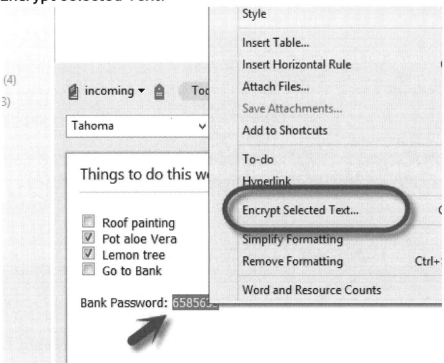

You'll be asked to enter a password and then re-enter to verify. You can also enter a hint to help you remember the password.

Evernote encrypts the text.

To unencrypt the text so you can read it, double-click on the padlock. You'll be prompted for the password. Enter the password and click OK. The text becomes unencrypted.

Be aware that if you move off the note, and then back to it, the padlock will reappear and you have to re-enter the password to unlock it.

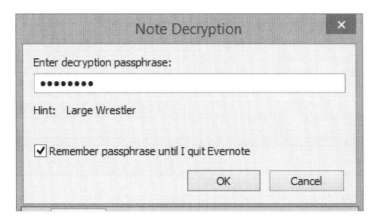

If you don't want to have to re-enter the password in the current Evernote session, just check the **Remember passphrase until I quite Evernote** box. When you return to the note, the padlock will be back, but double clicking it reveals the protected text.

Mac
To encrypt text in Evernote for Mac, select the text you want to encrypt (it can be the entire body of the note, but you cannot encrypt entire notebooks).

Once the text is selected, right click on it:

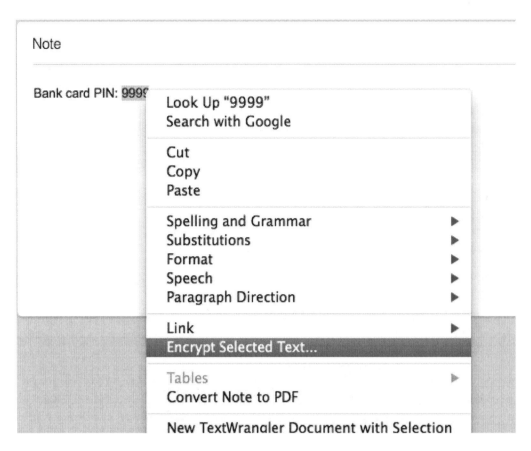

Note

Bank card PIN: 9999

Look Up "9999"	
Search with Google	
Cut	
Copy	
Paste	
Spelling and Grammar	▶
Substitutions	▶
Format	▶
Speech	▶
Paragraph Direction	▶
Link	▶
Encrypt Selected Text...	
Tables	▶
Convert Note to PDF	
New TextWrangler Document with Selection	

Select **Encrypt Selected Text** from the menu.

You need to enter a password and confirm the password.

You can also add a recovery question that will remind you of the password.

Click **OK** to encrypt the text.

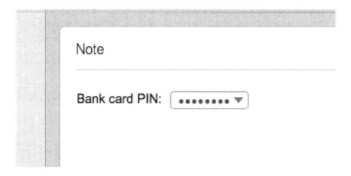

To unencrypt the text, click on the down arrow:

Select **Show encrypted text**, or **Decrypt text permanently**, whichever you want to do.

You'll be prompted for the password, and be shown your recovery question as an aid.

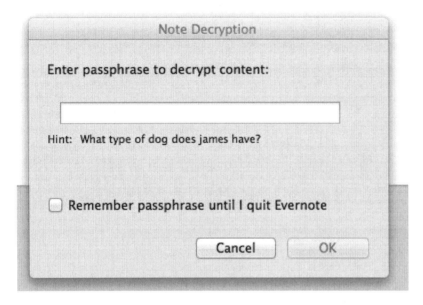

Type the password and press OK. You'll be able to view the encrypted text again.

Android
You cannot encrypt text on an Android device. However, you can view encrypted text by tapping the encryption box and typing the password.

iOS
You cannot encrypt text on an iOS device. However, you can view encrypted text by tapping the encryption box and typing the password.

Creating Notes by Sending emails to Evernote

When you sign up for an Evernote account, you are given a special email address that you can use to email yourself "notes".

Imagine receiving your flight booking details in your inbox. Forward it to your Evernote email address and your flight details will be saved as a note, and accessible from all of your digital devices.

The first thing you need to do is find your Evernote email address. We have covered this already, but let's recap.

In Evernote Web, open the Account Settings.

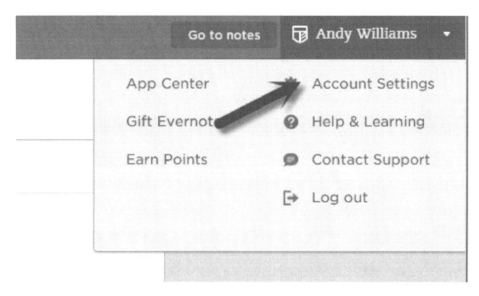

On the Account summary tab, you'll see a section like this:

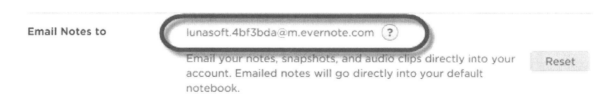

This shows you your Evernote email address, and anything you send to that email address will end up as a note. If you ever need to change your Evernote email address (like I do as I've just shown you mine), click the **Reset** button, and a new email will be created for you.

So, what notebook do these notes end up in? What is the title of the note? Can you add tags to these emailed notes?

I'll answer that in a moment, but first, let me remind you how to find your Evernote email address from the desktop versions of Evernote.

On **Evernote PC**, simply click on the help menu and select **Go to my Account Page**. This will open up your account page in a web browser (the same page you saw in Evernote Web) with your Evernote email address.

On a **Mac**, from the Evernote menu, select **Account Info....**

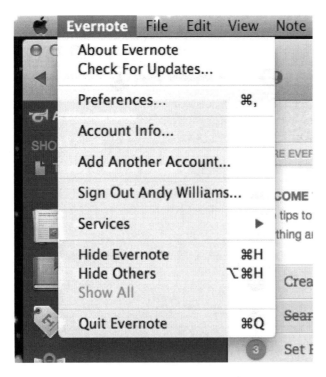

You'll see your Evernote email listed there:

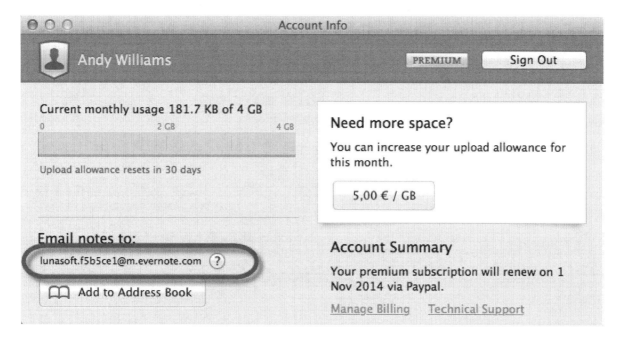

On **Android devices**, tap the menu (three vertical dots top right), and select **Settings**. At the top, your name is listed under **Account Info**. Tap your name. The **Account Info** screen opens, and your Evernote Email address is listed on that page.

On an **iOS device**, open the left sidebar and tap on your name (or the settings "cog" to the left of your name). Tap **General** from the **Settings** menu and then **Evernote Email Address**. You'll see your email address listed on that page, with a convenient **Copy to Clipboard** option.

OK, let's look at the options you have for sending emails to Evernote.

Here are the things to remember:

1. The subject line of your email becomes the note title.
2. The body of the email becomes the note.

Your subject line can also contain three different symbols:

1. Adding @ followed by the name of a notebook will send that email to that particular notebook. If this symbol is not found in the subject line, the note is sent to the default notebook.
2. Adding # followed by a tag will assign that tag to the note. You can include more than one tag (see example in a moment).
3. Adding ! followed by a date will set a reminder for the note.

For example, I've just received an email and need to reply to it, but don't currently have the information I need to answer the email. Therefore, I'll forward it to my Evernote account.

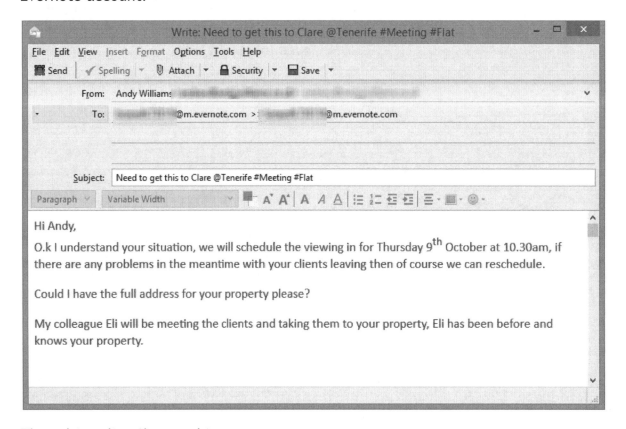

The subject line I've used is:

Need to get this info to Clare @Tenerife #Flat #Meeting

The first part "Need to get this info to Clare" will be used as the note title.

The note will be created in the notebook I have called "Tenerife", and the note will be tagged with two tags – Flat and Meeting.

Note that the tags and notebook MUST exist to be able to use these features in the subject line.

Here is the note after it arrived in Evernote.

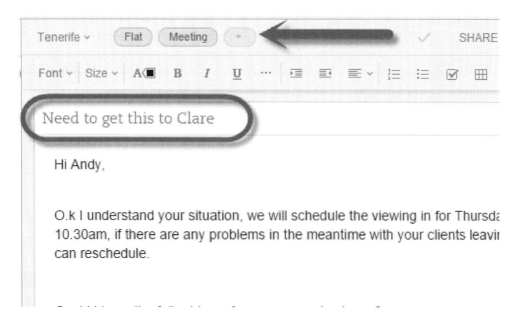

You can see the title of the note and the tags.

The only thing I didn't include in my email to Evernote was a reminder date.

If you want to include this, be aware that you cannot currently include a time for the reminder. The format for adding a reminder date is as follows:

!yyyy/mm/dd

For example, !2014/10/06 will set the reminder date for 6th October 2014.

You can also use:

!1week to set the reminder 1 week from today.

!sunday will set the reminder for the next Sunday.

!monday

!tuesday

.. and so on.

How to make Evernote templates/forms

Occasionally it's helpful to have a template or form that can be reused over and over again for entering information. For example, suppose you were a fish fanatic and wanted to keep records of the fish in your aquarium. You might like to have a template/form that you could fill in for each fish that you added to the aquarium. Your fish records might look something like this:

- Date Bought
- Supplier
- Cost of the fish
- Common name
- Scientific name
- Comments

Since you record the same information for each fish, wouldn't it be useful if you had a readymade form you could fill each time you bought a new fish, and file each as a separate note?

Unfortunately, Evernote does not have this type of template functionality built into it, but there is an application we can use to create templates called KustomNote.

We'll look at that in a moment, but first, if you have simple requirements for your templates/forms, there is a possible solution that does not require any third party applications.

My personal recommendation is to create a Notebook called Templates, where you can build this type of template and store it until it is needed. Here is a simple template I've created to record fishy information:

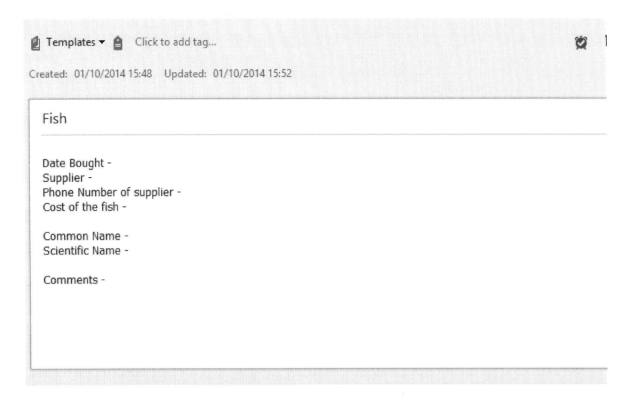

It's stored in a Notebook called Templates, which I could use for all of the forms & templates I wanted to create.

Now, when I buy a new fish, I could simply copy the template to my Aquarium notebook and edit it there. How you would copy it to the Aquarium notebook depends on the platform you are using. Let's look at each.

PC

With Evernote for PC, the process is incredibly easy.

Right click on the note template and select **Copy to Notebook**.

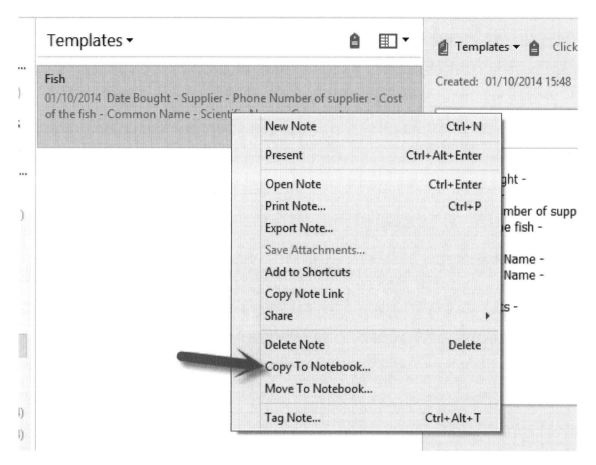

You'll be prompted for a Notebook to copy it to:

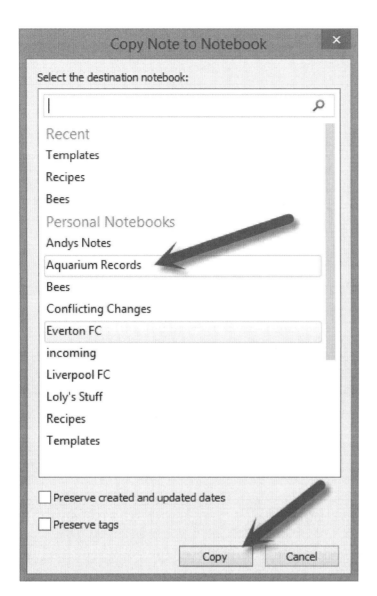

Click the Aquarium Records notebook, and click the **Copy** button. A copy of the template will then be saved to the Aquarium notebook, ready for filling in.

Mac
On the Evernote for Mac, CTRL + click on the template note and select **Copy to Notebook**. Choose the notebook from the list offered:

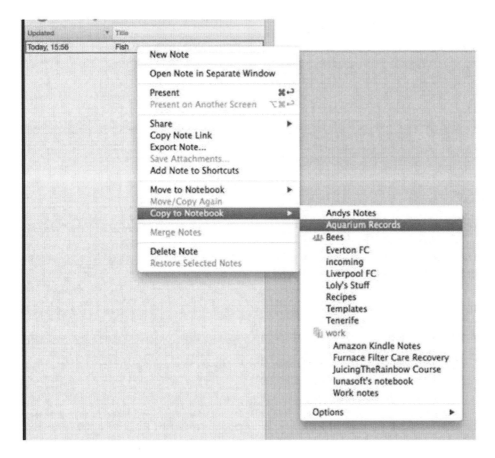

Since you are copying the note from one notebook to another, any tags you have added to your template note will be copied across with the new note.

Android

On an Android device, open the Template notebook and tap and hold the note you want to copy. From the menu that appears, select **Duplicate** and tap on the notebook you want to save in.

iOS

On iPad and iPhone, it's not quite as easy. You get a **Duplicate** menu item, but it duplicates in the same template notebook. That means you then need to move it to the Aquarium Records after it's been created.

To move the note on an iPhone or iPad, when the duplicate note opens, look for the Notebook name (top left on the screen) and tap that. You can then select the notebook you want to move it to.

KustomNote for better Evernote templates

KustomNote is a third party solution for creating templates in Evernote. You can find their website here:

https://kustomnote.com/

The idea behind this solution is that you can login to the KustomNote website (on your computer, or via a mobile app available for Android and iOS), and use pre-created templates to fill out the information. Once the information is completed in these templates, you "post" them to your Evernote account, and the information is saved as a note in your Evernote account.

You can sign up for an account at KustomNote, and as soon as you login, you'll have the opportunity to connect your Evernote account to KustomNote.

Clicking that button will take you to a consent screen, asking you to authorize KustomNote. This will grant KustomNote access to your Evernote account for 1 year.

Here is what you are authorizing, taken directly from the KustomNote website:

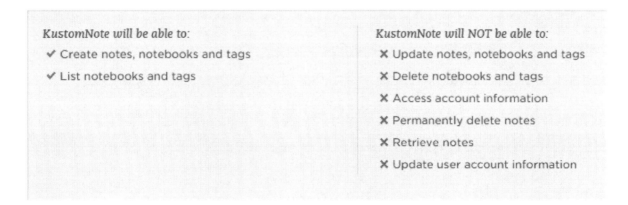

217

Upon authorization, you will be taken to a profile page, where you can fill out details about yourself, if you want to. Otherwise, you can use the menu on the left to start creating your first template (or using one someone else has created).

I'll leave you to explore KustomNote yourself, to see if it is of value to you. I'll just grab a template created by someone else and show you what happens as I fill in information and post it to my Evernote account.

I found a pre-made template for recording fish in an aquarium ;)

To make use of these templates created by other people, you just need to open the template and click the **Clone** button. You can then edit and fine tweak the template for your own use before saving it.

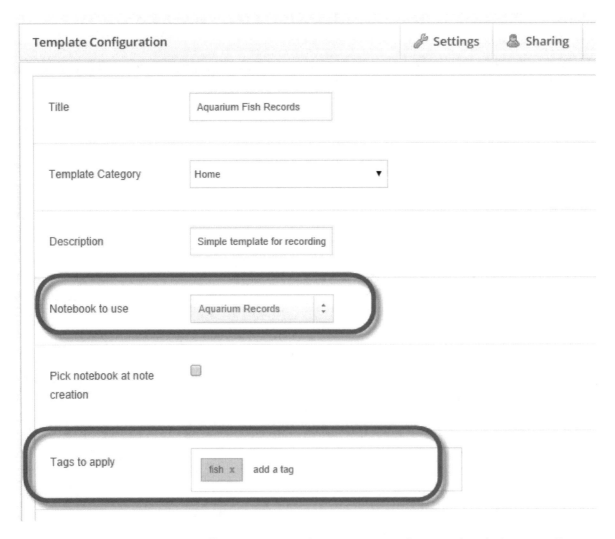

Each template you create allows you to choose a specific notebook in your Evernote account to use. You can also prefill tags to be included with each of these notes.

I've selected my Aquarium Records notebook, and tagged all entries with "fish".

Every time I fill in this form, the note will be tagged with "fish" and sent to my Aquarium Records notebook.

When you are happy with your form, save it. Now, whenever you click on **New Note** in the left sidebar, you'll be offered this template (and any others you have created):

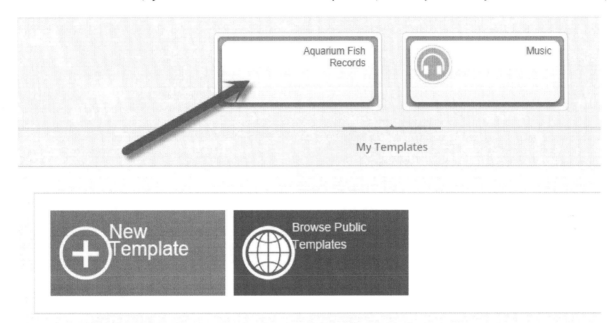

Clicking the **Aquarium Fish Records** button will open the form, ready to be filled:

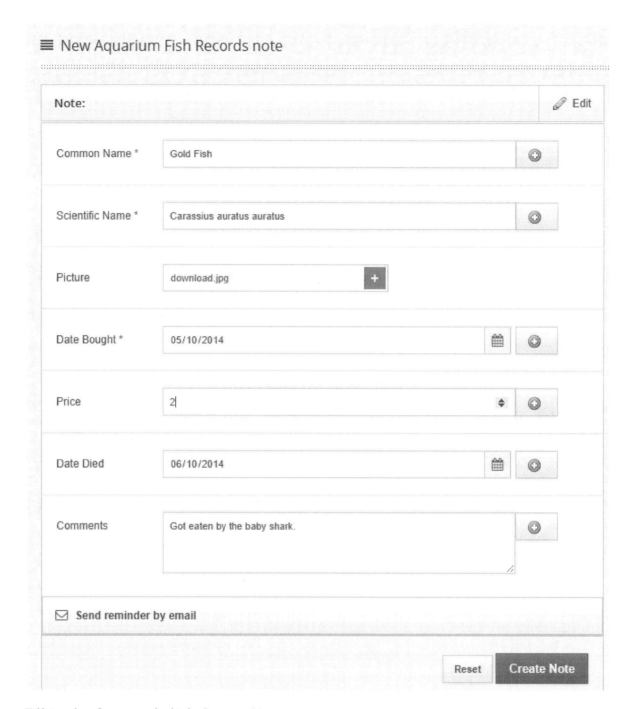

Fill in the form and click **Create Note**.

When you click the **Create Note** button, the information in this form is sent to your Evernote account.

I added a demo note using that form. You can see it in my list of notes in the Aquarium notebook:

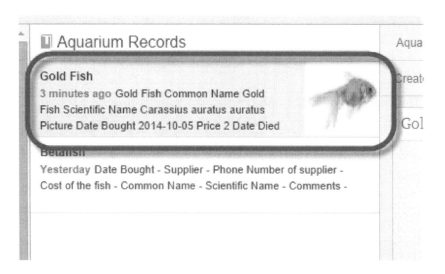

Aquarium Records

Gold Fish

3 minutes ago Gold Fish Common Name Gold
Fish Scientific Name Carassius auratus auratus
Picture Date Bought 2014-10-05 Price 2 Date Died

Betafish

Yesterday Date Bought - Supplier - Phone Number of supplier -
Cost of the fish - Common Name - Scientific Name - Comments -

The actual note itself has all of the information I entered into the form.

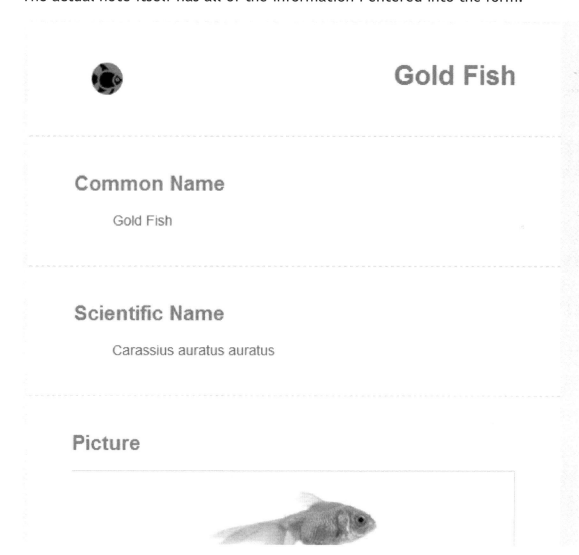

Gold Fish

Common Name

Gold Fish

Scientific Name

Carassius auratus auratus

Picture

KustomNote works very well, so if you need this type of template entry for your notes, do check it out. It starts off free, and for most people that is probably enough.

Using Tags

We've looked at tags earlier in the book, and how we can use them to organize our notes. Let's look at how we can insert, delete and manipulate tags.

Adding and deleting tags

As we saw earlier, tags can be used to help organize your notes. Adding them to a note is easy enough.

Let's look at Evernote Web first. If you want to add tags to an existing note, open the note. The toolbar at the top lists the notebook that the currently open note belongs to, and next to that are the tags:

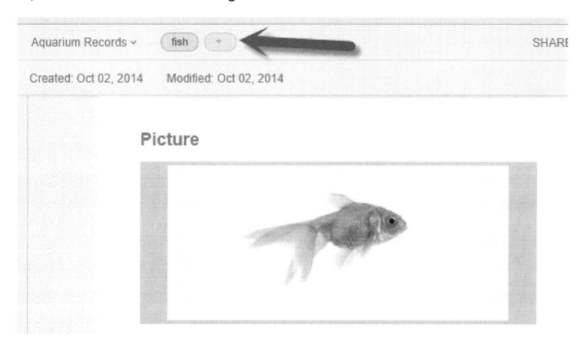

The note above has one tag – fish. To add another one, click the "+" button at the end of the tags, and that box just opens up, ready for you to type in a new tag.

When you have finished adding the new tag, press the return key on your keyboard and a new tag box will be created in anticipation of another tag. If you don't want to add any more, just click onto the note itself and the box will revert back to a "+" sign.

Any new tags you add to a note will be listed in your tags list:

223

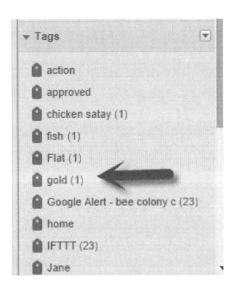

The same principles apply when adding tags to a newly created note, but the screen looks a little different:

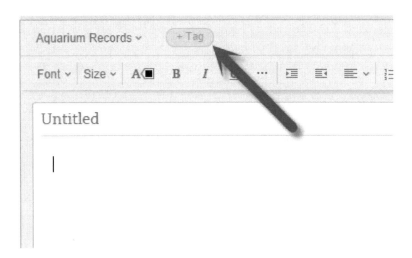

Just click into that box and begin typing.

Now, you may be wondering why you have that tag list in the left sidebar.

The answer is, so you can drag and drop tags from that list into a note. Just click and hold the mouse button on a tag you want to use for a note, and drag the tag over the note.

Drop it and the tag will be added to the note.

To delete any tag, simply click on it to select it, and press the delete key on your keyboard.

PC

Adding and deleting tags on the PC version of Evernote is almost identical to using the Evernote Web application. The tag area of the note looks slightly different, but functions in an identical manner:

To add a tag, click on **Click to add tag..**, or drag the tag from the tag list in the left sidebar and drop it onto the note.

To delete a tag, simply move your mouse over the tag and a small "x" appears in the tag. Click it to delete the tag.

Mac

If you are creating a new note, there is an obvious **click to add tags**:

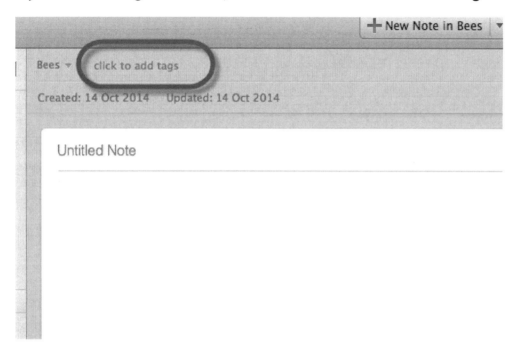

Simply click and type.

If you have existing notes that you want to add tag(s) to, Evernote for Mac may confuse you. When you open the note, the toolbar at the top shows existing tags, but does not show any obvious place to add new tags:

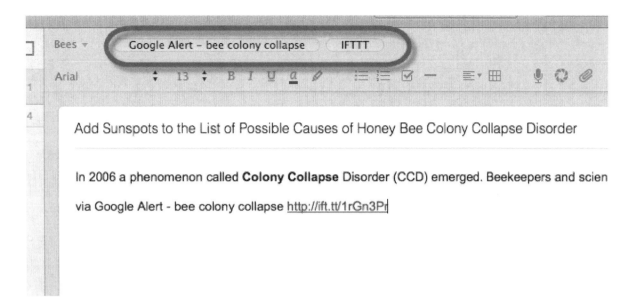

I've drawn a rectangle around existing tags. To add a new one, you simply need to click to the right of the last tag and start typing:

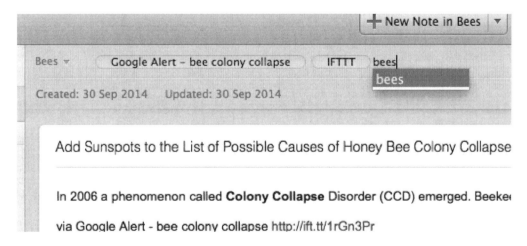

When you've entered the tag, press the Return key and the tag will be added.

If you have your tags visible in the left sidebar, you can also drag and drop tags from the list, directly onto your note. They will be added to the note.

To delete a tag, click on it and press the delete key on your keyboard.

Android
To add a tag to a note in the Android version of Evernote, open the note and then click on the information button:

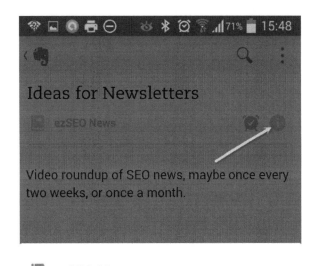

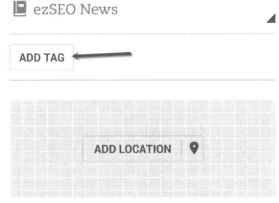

Now click the **Add Tag** button.

You'll be offered a complete list of tags to check, or you can type new ones in at the top of this list.

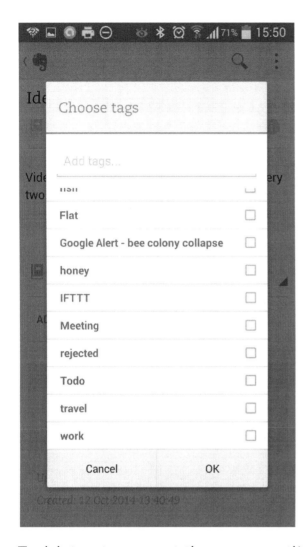

To delete a tag, repeat the process outlined above until you get to the screen that allows you to add tags. You'll see that each tag has a delete button which you can tap.

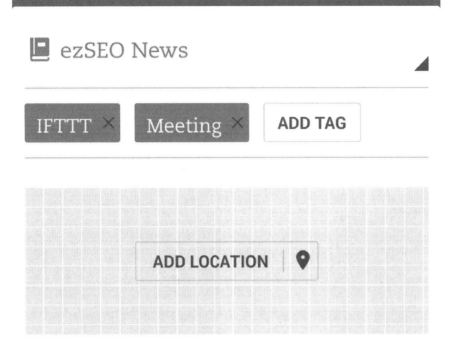

Tap the "X" to delete a tag.

iOS

To add a tag on iOS devices, open the note you want to add a tag to, and tap on the information button:

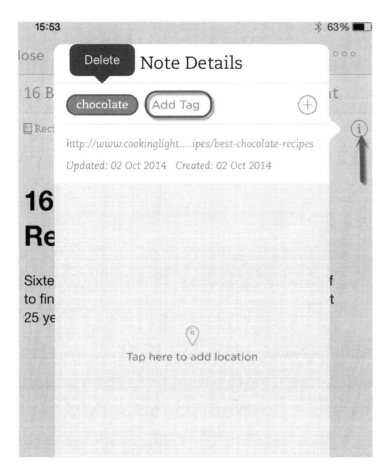

There is an **Add Tag** button that you can tap to add a tag. Tap and type your tags.

If you want to select a tag from your existing tags, tap the "+" inside the circle. This opens up a list of all tags in your account:

This screen scrolls vertically through your tags. You can use the search box at the top to find specific tags, or click the **Sort** button to sort by **Name** or **Count** (the number of times a tag has been used).

To delete a tag, open the note and tap the **Info** button.

Now tap the tag you want to delete and a **Delete** menu appears.

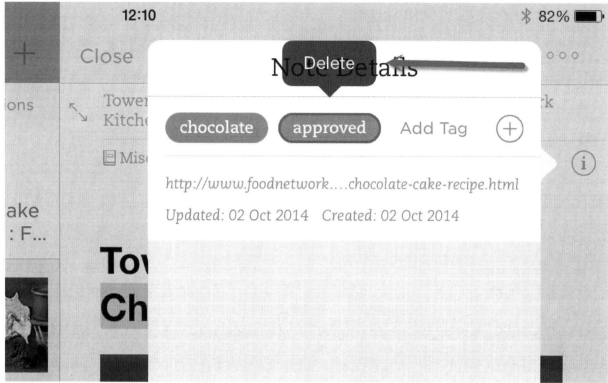

Tap **Delete** to remove the tag.

The order of Tags in the tag list

The tags in the left sidebar are listed in alphabetical order. However, you may have certain tags that you use more often, and therefore would prefer if they appeared near the top of the list.

You can do this by using special characters as a prefix to your tag. The order in which these special characters appear is as follows:

!

#

$

%

&

*

@

So, any tag with a ! prefix will appear first in the list of tags.

Any tag with a # prefix will appear after any tags with a ! prefix, but before any other tag, and so on.

Look at this tag list:

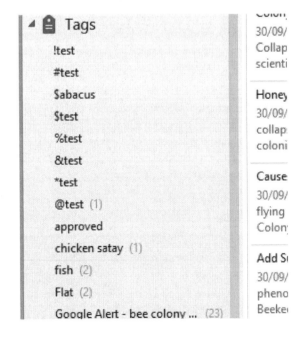

Notice how the tags using these prefixes appear before the tags without, and the prefixes are sorted in the order I mentioned above?

Also look at that list again. I have two tags prefixed with the $ symbol.

$test and $abacus.

The $abacus appears first, because with identical first characters ($), the sort order is then decided on the next character in the string, and "a" comes before "t".

Quickly finding all notes with a specific tag

We have already seen one way of returning all notes that use a specific tag – with the **tag:** operator.

e.g. **tag:chocolate**

This one will return all notes that have been tagged with chocolate. This is the recommended method in all versions of Evernote. Go back over the chapter on searching for notes if you need a refresher.

There are other ways to find all notes using a specific tag.

In the Evernote Web app, scroll down to the tag you are interested in, and click on it:

The search box in the toolbar at the top will change to include that tag, and all notes using that tag will be displayed in the results:

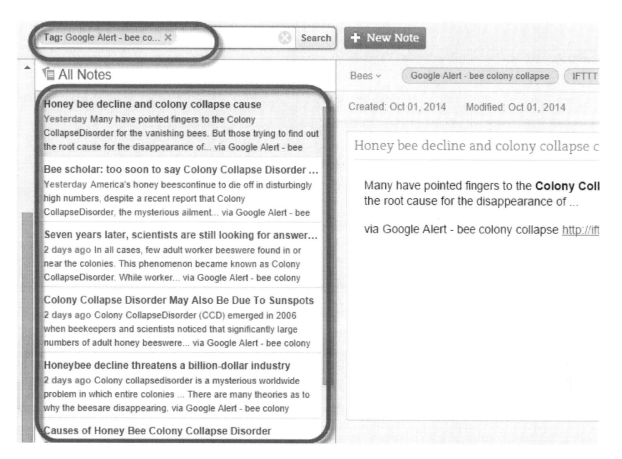

If you want to find all notes that have two or more tags in common, click the first tag to add it to the search box, then, holding the CTRL button on your keyboard, click the next tag you want to include. With each click, the new tag is added to the search box:

You can delete tags from the search box by clicking the "x" next to the tag.

PC
On the PC version of Evernote, everything works in a similar manner to the Evernote Web application.

Click on any tag to add it to the search bar. Hold the CTRL key as you click other tags if you want to add more than one tag to the search filter.

In addition, you can click on **Tags** in the sidebar to display a grid of all your tags:

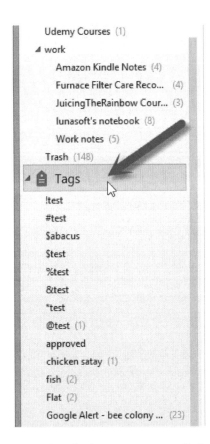

Double clicking on any of these tags in the grid will also open up the search to show those notes using that tag.

Mac
If you have the tags visible in the left sidebar, click on one. All notes that use that tag are shown to the right.

Android
On an Android device, open the left sidebar and tap on **Tags**. This opens a list of tags. Tap on the one you are interested in. All of the notes using that tag will be displayed.

iOS
On iOS devices, open the left sidebar, and tap on Tags.

You'll get a list of tags. Tap the one you are interested in viewing. All notes tagged with that tag will be listed.

Renaming tags

You can rename tags, and once renamed, all notes that used the original tag will be updated to use the newly renamed tag.

In the Evernote Web application, right click on the tag in the left sidebar, and select **Rename** from the popup menu:

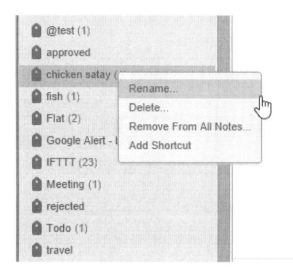

You can also delete tags from that menu, or remove that particular tag from all notes.

The final option in that menu is to add a shortcut to the tag. Shortcuts appear at the top of the left sidebar above the Notebooks section.

You'll see in the screenshot above that the shortcut to my fish tag has a "tag" icon next to it. You can also create shortcuts to notes and notebooks. I have one of each in my shortcuts. Notice the different icons used for tag, notes and notebooks.

Any tags listed in the shortcuts section can also be dragged and dropped onto a note to add the tag to that note.

Shortcuts to notes simply open that note when you click on the shortcut, and a shortcut to a notebook, opens that notebook.

PC

Renaming a tag in the PC version of Evernote is the same process as the Web version. Right click the tag in the left sidebar tag list, and select **Rename** from the menu:

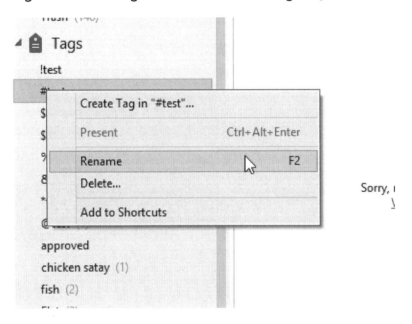

Notice you also have **Delete** and **Add to Shortcuts** options.

The **Present** (as in presentation) option in my screenshot is greyed out because there are no notes using that tag. If there were, I could select **Present**, and Evernote would create a presentation of the notes using that tag.

The option to **Create Tag in...** simply creates a nested tag inside the parent tag (the tag you right clicked).

You can also rename tags in the PC version by clicking **Tags** in the sidebar to reveal the grid of tags:

Right-clicking the tags on this screen allow you to rename, delete or add shortcuts.

Mac

On Evernote for Mac, if you have tags visible in the left sidebar, click on **Tags**. If you do not have them visible in the sidebar, click **Tags** in the **View** menu.

The tags screen will open, with a list of all tags.

Right-click the one you want to rename.

This menu gives you the option of renaming your tag. You can also delete it, or remove the tag from all notes.

Android
It's not currently possible to rename tags in the Android version of Evernote.

iOS
You can rename tags in the iOS version of Evernote. Open up the left sidebar, and tap on **Tags**.

On the Tags screen, tap on the **Edit** button top right:

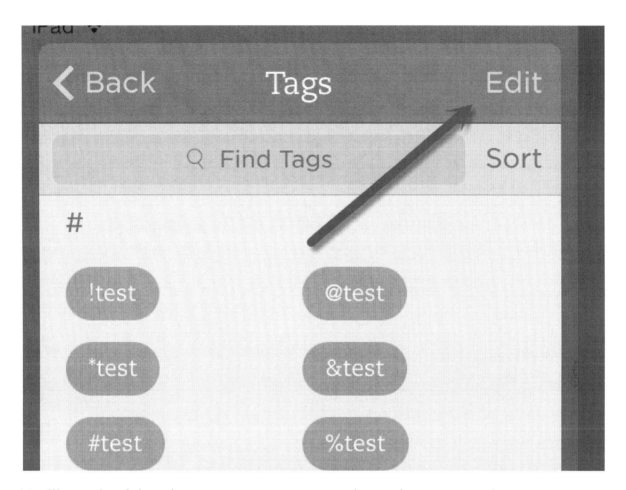

You'll see the delete button appear next to each tag, but you can also tap onto a tag, which then allows you to edit the tag:

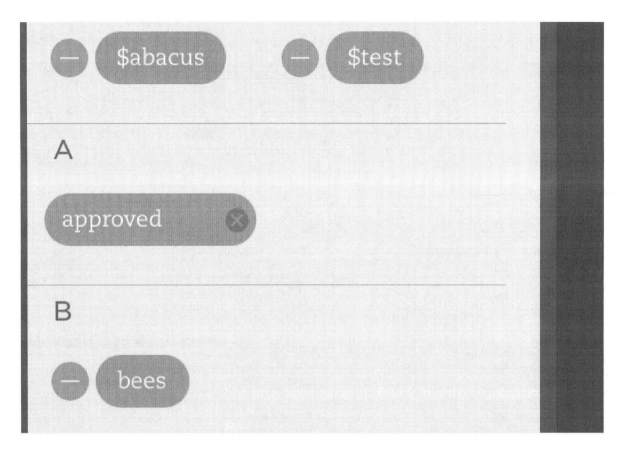

You cannot see the cursor in the screenshot above, but it's at the end of the word "approved". You can see the "approved" tag no longer has a delete button, as Evernote waits for me to rename the tag.

When a tag is renamed, all notes using that tag are updated with the new name.

Searching Notes

Evernote is designed to help you find things in as easy and intuitive manner as possible. Tags help a lot if you use them.

Do you want to find all notes related to your son? If you tagged all of those notes with your son's name, you can search for notes that use the tag.

There are usually different ways to search for most things, so let's start off by looking at simple searches, and we'll use Evernote Web for this, but the same principles apply to all versions of Evernote.

Suppose you want to find all chocolate recipes. You could use the search bar to search for:

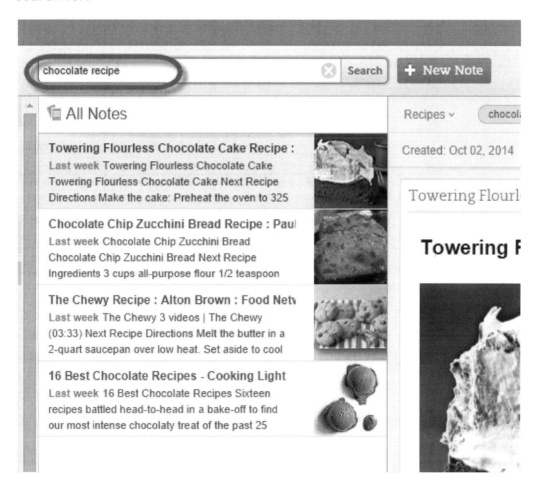

Whenever you search for something like this in Evernote, it will only match notes that contain ALL of the words you include in the search box.

Therefore, those notes that contain the words "chocolate" AND "recipe" are returned. You therefore don't need to (and it won't work anyway) use the specific

Boolean "AND" operator in Evernote search. All searches like this are "AND" searches.

What if you want to find all notes that contain the word chocolate but NOT recipe?

This is another example where BOOLEAN operators would seem natural, but they are not allowed in Evernote.

Instead, Evernote has an elegant solution. We'd search for:

chocolate –recipe

The "-" sign before the word **recipe** tells Evernote that we don't want notes containing the word **recipe**.

Therefore that search means, find all notes that contain the word chocolate, but do not contain the word recipe.

As we saw earlier, Evernote allows us to add tags to notes. These help organize our notes, and we can search directly using tags.

For example, if we had used "chocolate" and "recipe" as two different tags, we could:

1. Click on the "chocolate" tag in the left sidebar list, and all notes tagged with "chocolate" would be shown.
2. Click on the "recipe" tag in the left sidebar list, and all notes tagged with "recipe" would be shown.
3. CTRL + click the "chocolate" tag AND the "recipe" tag, and all notes that are tagged with "chocolate" AND "recipe" will be shown.

Of course, you may have a notebook called recipes, so all you'd need to do is search that notebook for chocolate. That's easy too.

Click into the search bar, and then click the **Recipes** notebook in the sidebar. The search box is updated to include **Recipes:**

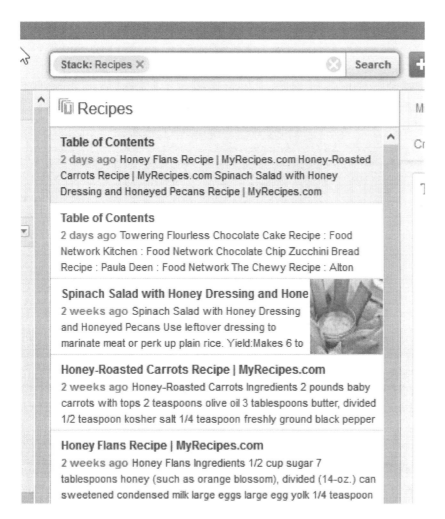

The search results list all recipes in that notebook. However, if I type the word chocolate into the search box AS WELL (and click the search button):

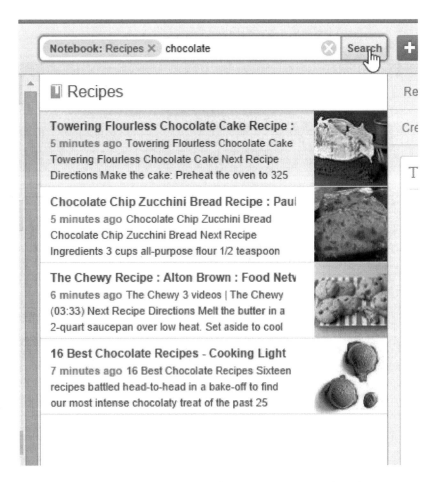

I know end up with notes in the **Recipes** notebook containing the word chocolate.

For any set of search results, you can order the search results using the **View Options** button at the bottom of the list:

Order the results by date created, date updated, or alphabetically.

This is great, but what if I am using "chocolate" as a tag? In that case, I don't need to type the word chocolate into the search box at all.

Instead, I can click on the chocolate tag in the tag list in the left sidebar and that adds the tag to the search box:

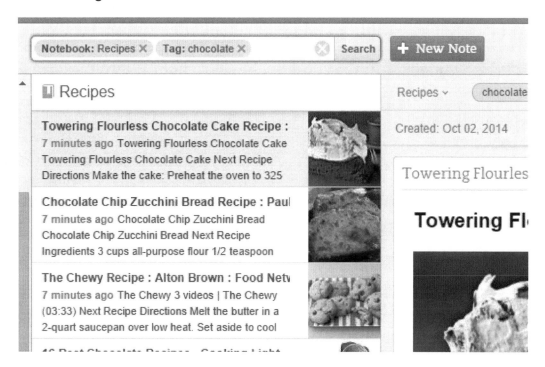

In the test database I am using for this book, it doesn't matter whether I:

1. Search for "chocolate",
2. Search in the **Recipes** notebook for "chocolate",
3. Search in **Recipes** notebook with the **chocolate** tag, or
4. Just search for the **chocolate** tag.

All four of those searches return the same set of 4 recipes.

However, as the number of notes grows, you may need one or other of these formats to pull out the information you want.

As an example, look at this search for "honey":

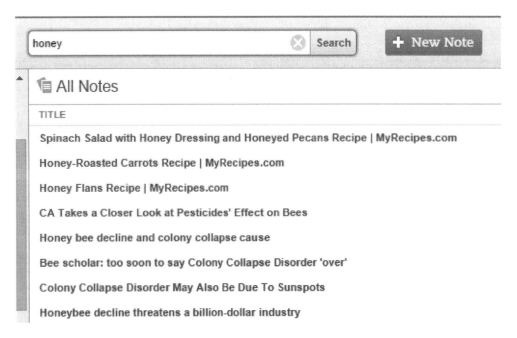

Some of those notes containing the word honey are in the **Recipes** notebook, while others are in the **Bees** notebook.

If I only wanted see honey reference related to bees, I'd:

1. Clear the search box.
2. Click the **Bees** notebook in the sidebar.
3. Type **honey** into the search box.
4. Press the Return key on the keyboard, or click the **Search** button.

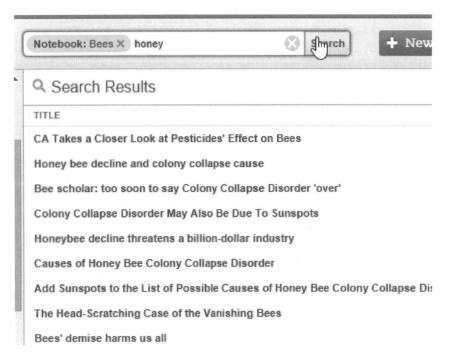

Now I just have the **honey** notes related to bees.

I can change the search to use the **Recipes** notebook instead if I want. To do this, click into the search box and it will expand downwards.

Click on the current notebook **Bees** in the menu, and select **Recipes** from the new sub-menu.

This will change the search to only include the **Recipes** notebook:

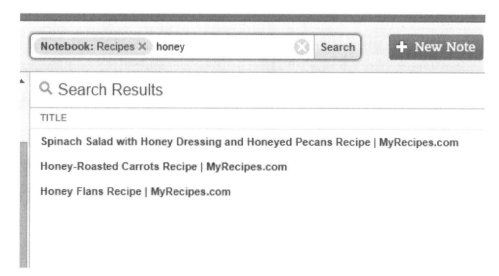

I now have a list of all recipes that include honey.

These simple searches using keyword, tag and/or notebook will be all most people need. However, Evernote search is much more powerful than that, so before we look at how we can extract just about anything from our Evernote database, let's just quickly look at the search boxes in the PC and Mac versions of Evernote, as these are a little different.

PC
On Evernote for PC, the search box is visible in the toolbar, top right.

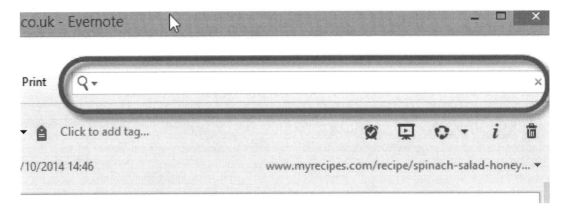

You can start off by searching with a simple keyword in that search box:

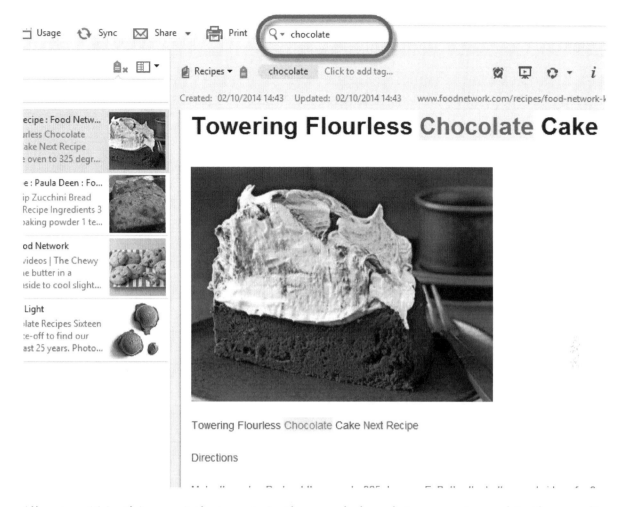

All notes (4 in this case) that contain the word chocolate are returned in the results. In addition, the word chocolate is highlighted in the visible note. Selecting a different note from the search results will display that note, again with the search word highlighted.

If I now click on a notebook in the left sidebar, the **chocolate** keyword is deleted from the search box, which now just filters notes in my chosen notebook. Here I clicked on my **Recipes** notebook.

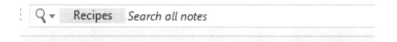

The same applies to clicking a tag. Any keyword search will be deleted, and replaced with a search for that tag.

If you want to search for notes that are tagged with two or more tags, you can hold down the CTRL key and click on the tags you want. This will populate the search box with the tags you select:

What if you want to search for a specific tag within a specific notebook?

Well, one way of doing it is to use operators, which we'll look at in a minute. The other is to select the notebook from the sidebar, and then hold the CTRL key and click on one or more tags.

Another way is to click on the notebook in the sidebar, and then use the **Filter by Tag** option at the top of the search results window. This is activated by clicking the small luggage tag:

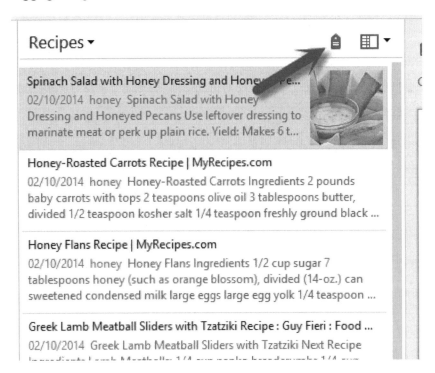

On clicking, you'll see a list of tags used by the notes in that notebook:

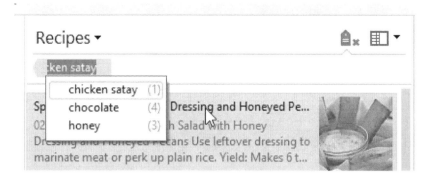

You can then click on the tag you are interested in. Note that each tag has a number in brackets after it. That indicates how many notes are using that tag.

If you want to filter by more than one tag, you can do that too. After adding your first tag to the filter, you'll see this:

Click that and if there are any possible tags (in other words, if a note has the first tag you selected AND another), then those other tags will be displayed.

Mac

To do a simple search on the Mac, type the word into the search box:

All notes that contain the word chocolate are shown in the list. You'll also notice that the word chocolate has been highlighted in the note body. You only see one in the screenshot above, but every instance of the word chocolate is highlighted in an identical manner.

To search for chocolate within a specific notebook, first search for "chocolate" as shown above. Now click your mouse into the search box, and it will expand downwards:

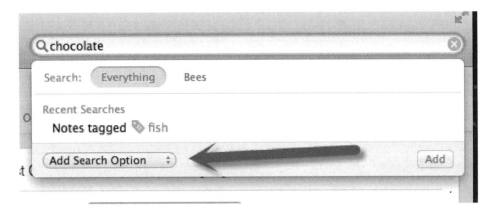

Click on the **Add Search Option** (you can use this to add layers to your search, refining the search):

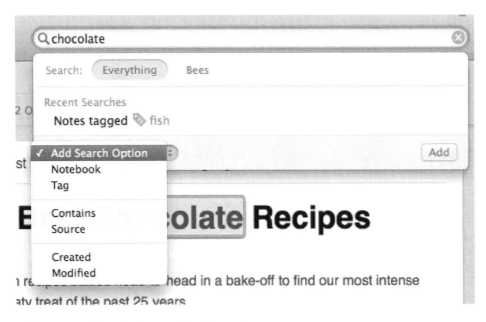

Select **Notebook** from the drop down menu.

You can then choose which notebook you want to restrict your search to:

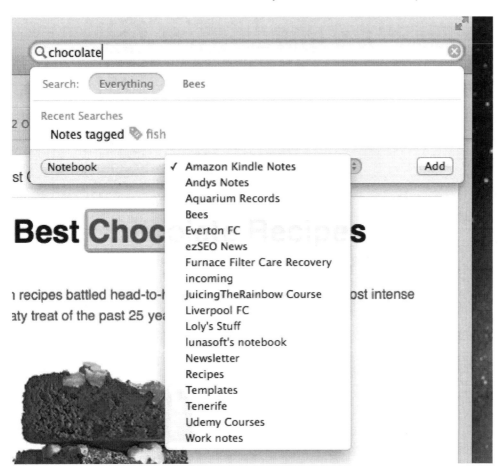

If I click on **Recipes** and then the **Add** button, my search ends up looking like this:

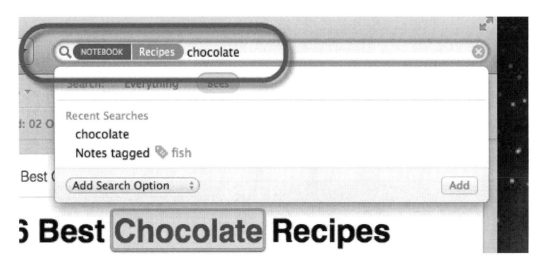

Best Chocolate Recipes

Evernote is searching in the **Recipes** notebook for notes containing the word **chocolate**.

If I used the tag **chocolate** on my notes in the **Recipes** notebook, I could search like this:

Best Chocolate Recipes

To achieve that search, I didn't type in any keyword. I simply used the **Add Search Option** button to select my **Recipes** notebook and then used the **Add Search Option** again to select **Tag**, and choose my **chocolate** tag:

This **Add Search Options** is an excellent way to build up a search.

Search Operators for power searchers

The most powerful way to search in Evernote on all platforms is to use operators.

The three I find most useful are:

notebook: This searches a particular notebook.

tag: This searches for a particular tag.

any: This searches for notes containing any of the words you specify in the search string.

We'll look at a more comprehensive list later, but let's look at examples of how to use these thee operators. I'll use Windows in my examples, but these will work on all platforms.

If I want to search my **Bees** notebook, I'd type this in the search box:

notebook:bees

This is how Evernote for Windows displays this in the search box:

See how it added the Bees notebook, with an "x" next to it for easy deletion.

OK, let's use the tag operator in a search.

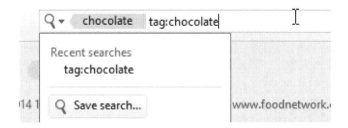

By typing in **tag:chocolate**, I've filtered out only those notes that have been tagged with chocolate.

I can modify this even more by adding other operators, or by including a search term in the search box:

I've now pulled out those notes tagged with **chocolate**, and including the word cake:

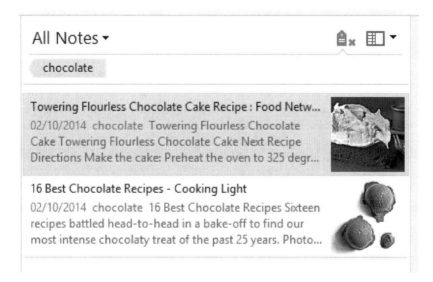

However, what if I wanted notes tagged with chocolate that were not recipes for cakes?

I can use the "-" symbol to exclude items in a search.

Let's look for chocolate tagged items that do not mention cake:

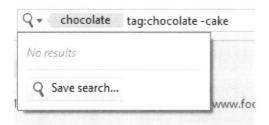

My search results are now different:

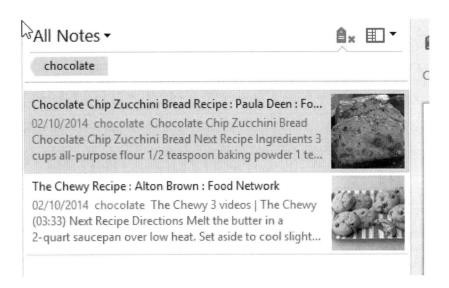

We can use the "-" on tags too.

What if I wanted to pull out all of the notes in my **Recipes** notebook, but not those tagged with chocolate:

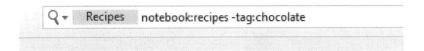

Searching with any:

When you search with two or more words, you are searching for notes that contain all of those words. Remember we mentioned earlier that the default search in Evernote is like a Boolean AND search.

e.g. If I type chocolate zucchini into the search box, only those notes with chocolate AND zucchini in them will be shown.

If I want to show notes that contain EITHER chocolate OR zucchini, I can use the any: operator.

any:chocolate zucchini

This will return notes that contain any of the words after the any: operator, in this case chocolate OR zucchini.

You can even use the **any:** operator with tags:

any: tag:chocolate tag:honey

This search will return notes that are tagged with either honey or chocolate.

Here is another example. If I want to search for notes in the **Bees** notebook that contain the words "scientist" OR "scholar". I can type this:

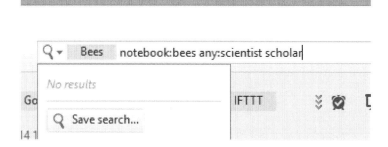

This search uses the **any:** operator to tell Evernote to include notes with **scientist** or **scholar** in them, but only from the **Bees** notebook.

Think of the **any:** operator as a way of forcing a Boolean OR search.

Using "-" in Search
As we've seen, the minus symbol "-" can be used to exclude specific words or tags in the search results.

Let's say you want to return notes that do not include the word "honey". You could search for this:

-honey

Let's search the **Bees** notebook for notes that do not include the word honey:

notebook:bees -honey

Or maybe I want to pull out notes from the **Recipes** notebook that are NOT tagged with honey:

notebook:recipes -tag:honey

Searching for an exact phrase with quotes
If you want to search for an exact phrase, enclose the phrase in quotes.

"honey bees" will only return notes that include the exact phrase **honey bees**.

Using Wildcards in Search
The asterisk symbol * is a wild card and represents one or many characters unknown.

It can be used when we're not sure of part of a search phrase. For example, if I wanted to find a recipe in my database for zucchini, but cannot remember how to spell zucchini, I could search for:

zuc*

Evernote then returns any note containing "zuc" followed by any (or none) other characters in the word. This isn't the best example for using a wildcard in search.

A better example is in searching for specific media types. You can search for notes with images using the following operators:

resource:image/png

This will find notes with PNG image files.

resource:image/jpeg

This returns notes that contain Jpeg images.

resource:image/gif

This returns notes that contain GIF images.

What if I know I want to find a note with an image, but don't know what format the image is?

This is where a wildcard can help.

I could return all notes with images by using a wild card:

resource:image/*

Evernote just looks for "resource:image/" with any additional characters, so PNG, JPEG and GIF are all returned.

Similarly, you can return all audio notes with a wild card:

resource:audio/*

Remember audio files can be different file types too, but this is elegantly handled by the wildcard.

Searching reminders

There are three search operators we can use to specifically search for notes with reminders. All three really need the * wildcard to make them useful.

The first is **remindertime:** and this searches for the date and time of the reminder. Clearly, if you need to search for a reminder, you probably don't know the date and time of the reminder, so by adding an * wildcard to the search, we can return ALL notes that have date and time set for a reminder.

In Evernote Web, it looks like this:

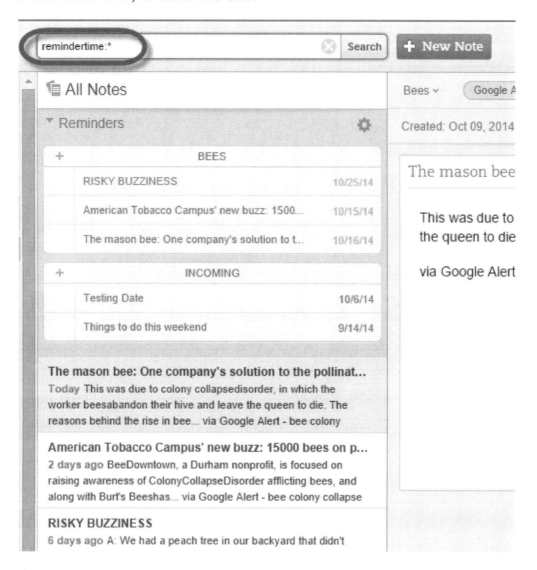

If you want to search for a reminder that you know is a week or so in the future, you could search for something like this:

remindertime:day+5

This will return all reminders set at least 5 days into the future.

The second operator for reminders is the **reminderdonetime:** which shows notes with reminders that have been marked as done/complete. Again, we use the * wildcard to show all notes where reminders are marked as done.

Here is that search in Evernote Web:

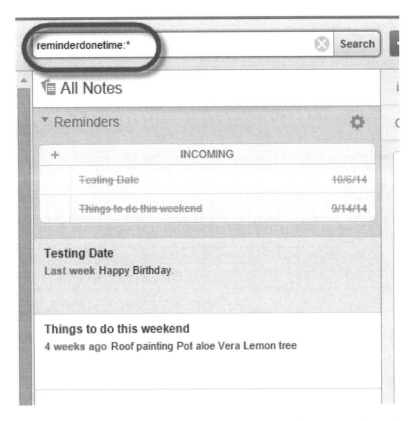

The final operator we can use to search reminders is **reminderorder:** which again needs the * wild card to be useful.

This operator will search for all notes that have a reminder set, irrespective of whether it has been marked as done or not. Here is that search in Evernote Web:

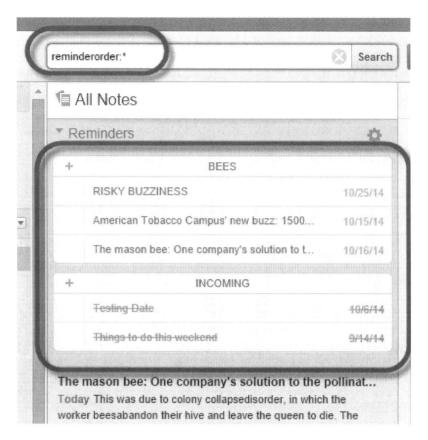

Notice that the list of reminders is split into two groups. Those that have been marked as done are at the bottom, and have a line through them. Those that have not yet been marked as done are at the top.

Saved searches

Whenever you create a search string that you know you'll want to use later, you can save it. Then, when you need to search for the same thing again, it's already entered and you can select it from a list.

Let's look at saving and reusing searches in Evernote Web first.

In the search box at the top, type in a search:

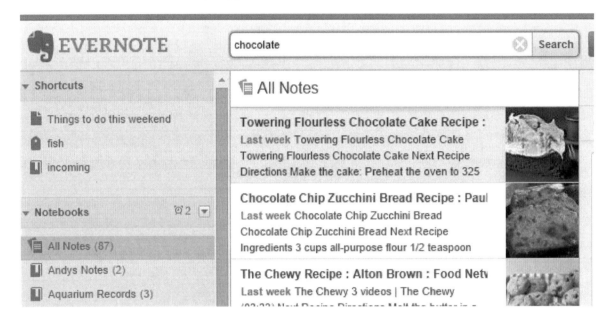

Now click back into the search box and the menu expands downwards:

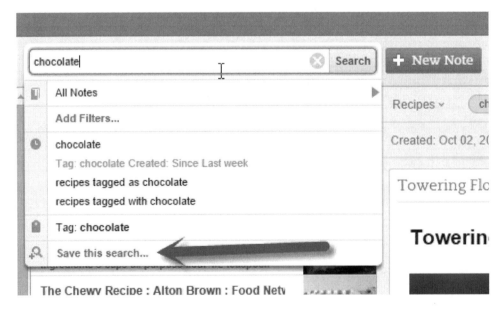

Click on the **Save this search...** option at the bottom and you'll be prompted to name the search.

To keep the name of my saved search unique from the search term (so you can spot it in the next screenshot), I've called my saved search **Chocolate saved search**.

To reuse a saved search, click into the search box to expand the menu:

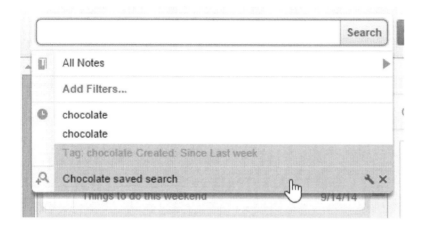

You can see the saved search at the bottom of the menu. Click on it to reuse that search.

Also note that when you mouse over the saved search, two icons appear to the right. These are the "edit search" and "clear search" features.

Edit search allows you to rename your saved search.

Clear search actually deletes the saved search.

OK, let's look at this feature in Evernote for PC.

PC
The first thing I want to show you is the drop down menu in the PC version of Evernote. You drop this down by clicking into the search box.

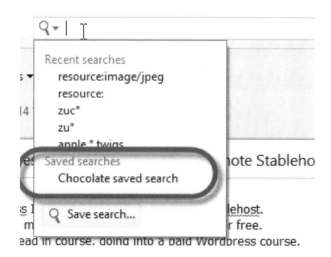

Notice how saved searches made in Evernote Web are synchronized to all other instances of Evernote you are using. The searches you save will be available on all of your devices.

In case you didn't read the Evernote Web section, let's create and then reuse a saved search.

After typing "chocolate cake" into the search box and pressing return, I can see the search results. If I want to save this search to reuse in the future, all I need to do is to click again into the search box to display the drop down menu:

Then click the **Save Search** button.

You'll be asked to confirm the saved search name and the actual query you want to save:

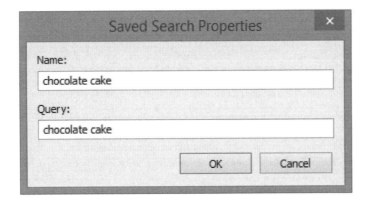

I'll change the name of the saved search a little so it is different from the query.

To reuse a saved search, click on the search box to display the drop down menu:

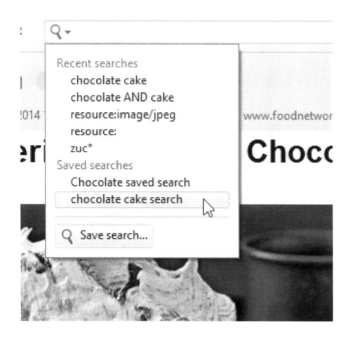

The chocolate cake search is listed with any other saved searches. To reuse it, just click on it.

To edit or delete a saved search, right click on the one you want to edit/delete:

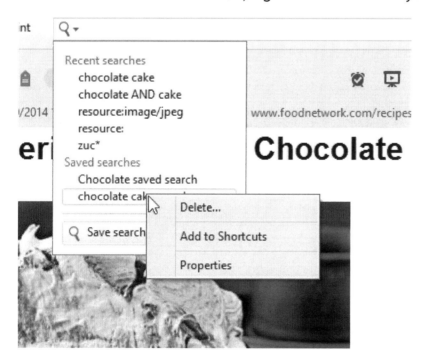

There is an option to delete the saved search, add it to your shortcuts (remember those appear top left of the sidebar), or access the properties, which simply gives you access to the search name and query so you can edit them.

Mac

To save a search on the Mac version of Evernote, you need to venture into the menus of Evernote. It's not very intuitive.

Here is the process:

1. Carry out your search.
2. Go to **Edit** -> **Find** -> **Save Search**.

You'll be prompted for a name for your search.

When you have saved searches, you can see them listed when you click into the search box:

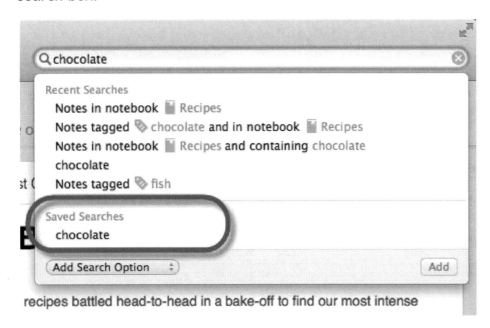

To edit the name of a saved search, or delete it altogether, move your mouse over the saved search in the menu:

You'll see the **Edit** button appear. Click it and you'll get the following dialogue box:

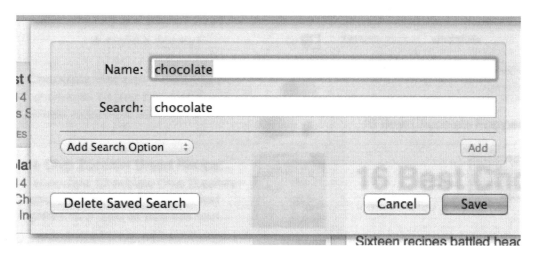

You can edit the name, or the search criteria from this screen. Also, bottom left is a **Delete Saved Search** button to get rid of unwanted saved searches.

Android
Saved searches work a little differently on Android devices. Rather than save the search in the Evernote interface, it adds an icon to your home screen that you can tap to re-run those searches.

To create a saved search on Android, carry out the search, then select **Add to Home Screen** from the menu.

Saved searches on Android do not sync across other platforms.

iOS
On iOS devices, you can create a saved search as follows:

1. Carry out your search.
2. In the search results screen, tap the save search button:

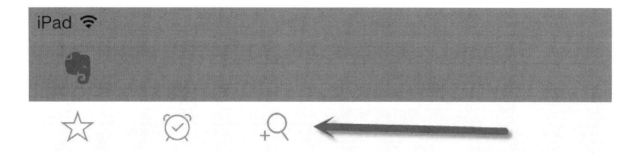

You'll be prompted to enter a name for the search.

When you go back to search again, you'll see your saved searches listed:

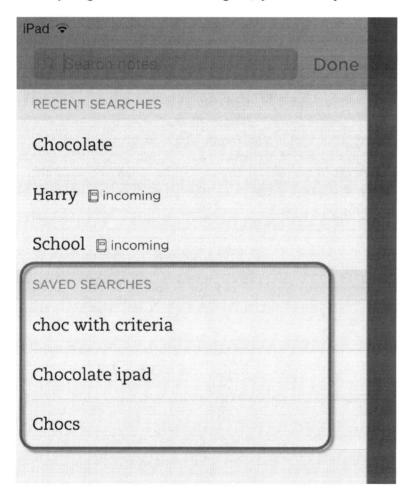

Just tap on one to run the search.

To delete a saved search, swipe the search from right to left, and tap on the delete button. You can also use this swipe gesture to delete "recent searches".

The full list of Search operators

There are a number of other search operators available to us. This section will look briefly at them.

Intitle: returns notes with the specified word in the title of the note.

e.g. to search for all notes that have the word chocolate in the title:

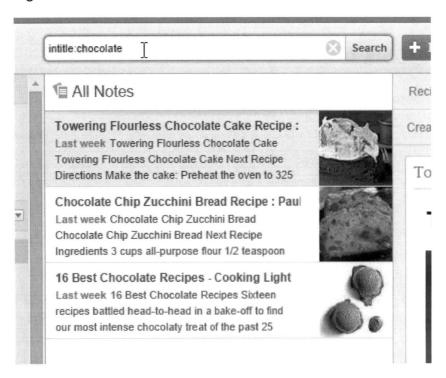

Created: allows you to search for notes created over a specific period of time or on a date if you know the date.

The date format is YYYYMMDD.

You can also use dates relative to today, so **created:day-1** searches yesterday, and **created:week-1** searches for notes created within the last week.

If I type **created:week-1** into the search box,

And press return, Evernote Web changes it to:

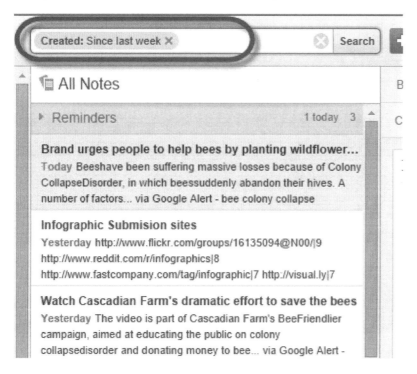

Evernote then displays those notes created in the last week.

Updated: allows you to search for notes that were updated over a specific period of time. Like the **created:** operator, this is probably most useful using **day-1** or **week-1** parameters:

Evernote changes this when I hit the return key:

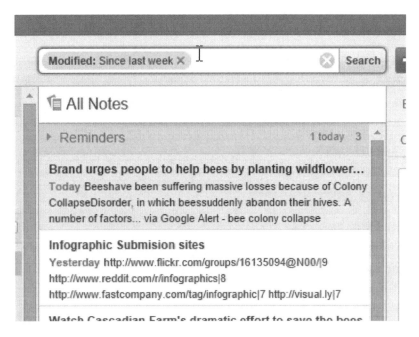

This then displays note that were updated/modified in the last week.

Notebook: Search for notes in a particular notebook.

To only display notes in my **Bees** notebook, I can type in **notebook:bees**

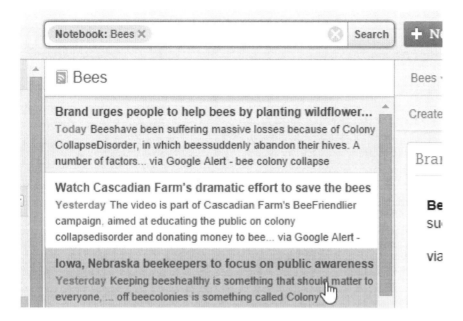

Tag: Find notes with a specific tag.

If I want to find those notes that use the tag **chocolate**, I'd type **tag:chocolate**

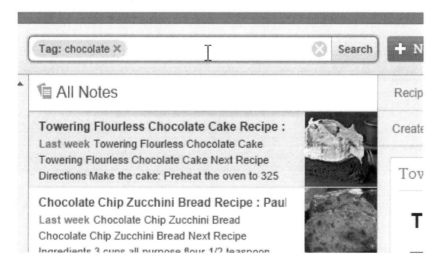

-tag: Find notes that don't use this tag.

Suppose I want to find all notes in the Recipe notebook except those that are tagged with **honey**. I can type:

notebook:recipes -tag:honey

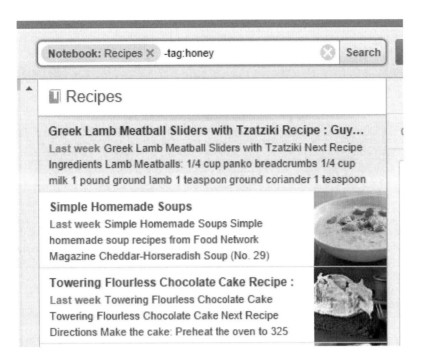

Any: This operator will return notes that include ANY of the search terms.

any: chocolate recipe

Note that there is a space between the colon and the first word.

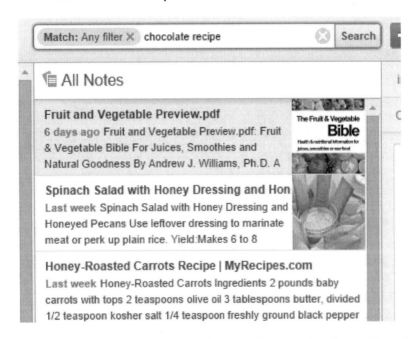

I can see the first item in the results is a book, unlike the others which are recipes. I can modify my search to add **notebook:recipes** like this:

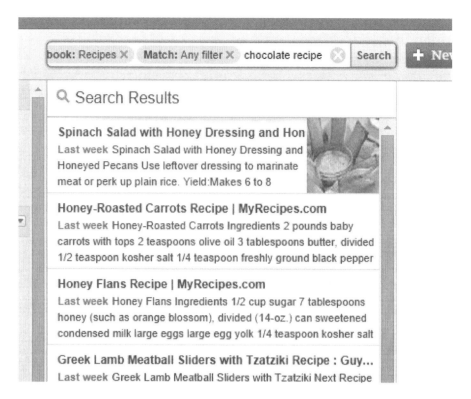

As we saw earlier, you can also use the any: operator with tags, so:

any: tag:chocolate tag:honey

.. will return and note tagged with **honey** or **chocolate**.

Resource: Will find notes of a specific media type.

E.g., **resource:image/png** will return notes with PNG images.

If you want to return notes with any kind of image, you can use the wildcard for the image type, so it becomes **resource:image/***

When you hit the return key, Evernote modifies the way the search is displayed, with **resource:image/*** becoming:

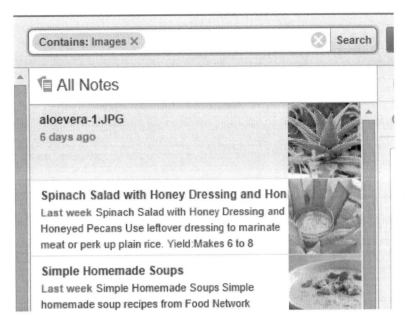

Source: This operator returns notes created with the stated source. The only time I use this is to find notes created on my mobile devices. I can do this with the following search:

Source:mobile.*

In Evernote Web, when you press the return key that becomes:

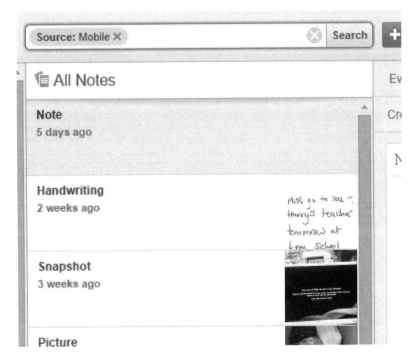

Todo: This will find any notes that contain checkboxes ("todo lists").

You use this operator by specifying true or false as the parameter. The parameter refers to whether the checkboxes are checked or not.

E.g. **todo:true** returns all notes that contain a checkbox that is checked, and this is changed in Evernote Web to:

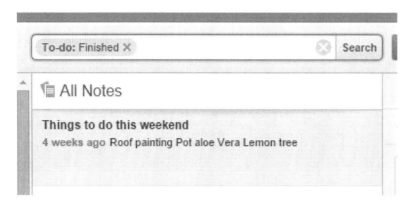

Whereas **todo:false** returns those notes that contain at least one checkbox that is unchecked. In Evernote Web, this becomes:

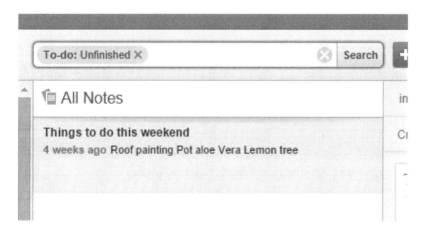

You will notice that in those last two screenshots, the same note was returned in both cases. That means the note contains some checkboxes that have been checked, and other(s) that have not been checked. I can confirm this by looking at the note:

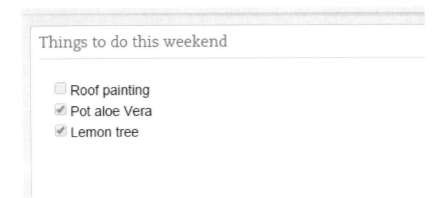

Encryption: This allows you to find notes that contain an encrypted element. You don't need to supply any parameters for this operator, simply type:

encryption:

Evernote web changes this to:

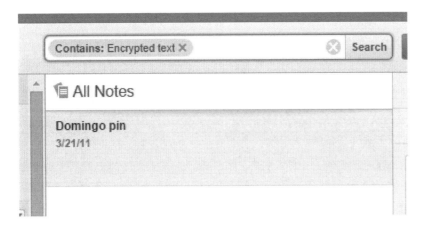

Latitude: Allows you to search for notes created at a specific latitude.

The parameter for latitude is a number from -90 to 90

e.g. **latitutde:28** will return all notes where the latitude is greater than 28. You can also use the "-" operator like this:

-latitude:28

This returns all notes created at a latitude less than 28.

If you want to find notes created at latitude 28, you could search for:

latitude:28 -latitude:29

This will find notes created where the latitude is greater than 28 AND less than 29.

I know that my latitude is 28.x, so I can search for notes created at my present location using this search.

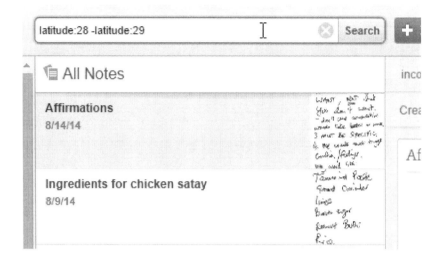

Longitude: Allows you to search for notes created at a specific longitude.

The parameter for longitude is a number from -180 to 180

The longitude operator works in the same way as the latitude one.

Miscellaneous

This section includes a few other features of Evernote that you might find useful. The first one is only currently available on the Windows version of Evernote.

Windows Import folders

This feature allows you to set up folder monitoring on your Windows computer. Any new documents that are added to these watched folders are automatically imported into Evernote.

To set this up, you need to be running the Windows version of Evernote. This feature is not currently supported on Mac.

From the **Tools** menu, select **Import Folders**:

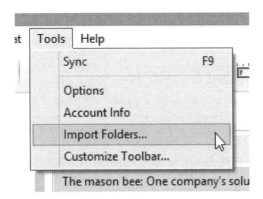

This opens up the **Import Folders** dialogue box:

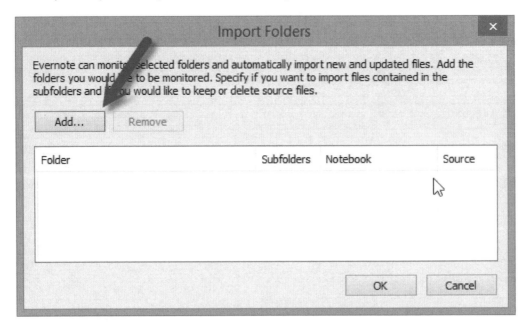

To start watching a folder, click the **Add** button. You can then use the Windows **Browse Folders** dialogue box to search for and select folders to watch.

Once you add a folder, it appears in the **Import Folders** screen:

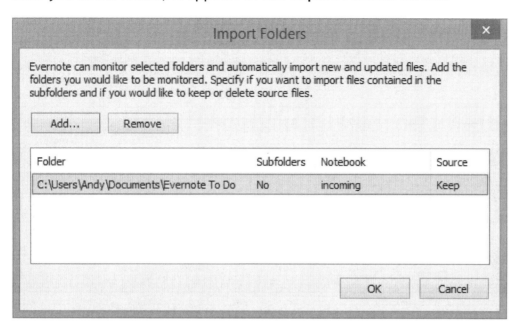

To remove the watched folder, just select it and click the **Remove** button.

The **Import Folders** screen shows a few attributes for each watched folder. These are:

1. Whether to watch sub-folders or not (default is no).
2. Which Notebooks to add these items to (default notebook is selected when you set up the watched folder).
3. Whether to keep the source, or delete it, once it is imported into Evernote.

You can make changes to these attributes directly in this table. Just click the value you want to change. For example, if I want to watch subfolders as well, I need to change the **No** to a **Yes**. By clicking directly on the **No**, I get the option to change it:

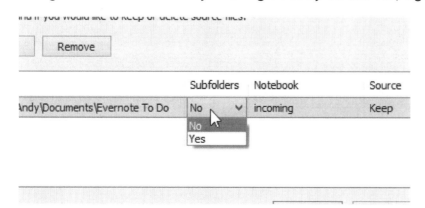

If you want to change the Notebook, click on the currently selected notebook and you'll be offered a list of all notebooks in your account:

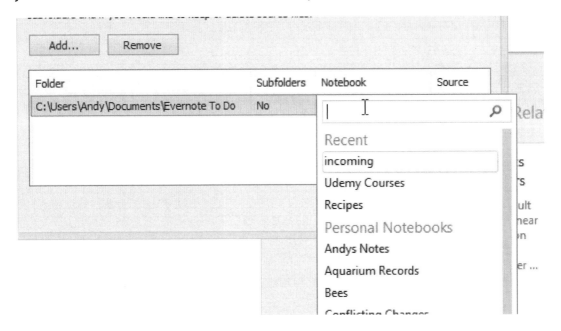

If you want to delete source documents as they are imported, change the source from **Keep** to **Delete**. This will then delete the item from the watched folder after it is imported into Evernote.

So what do the imported notes look like?

Well, I added three documents to my watched folder, so I could show you.

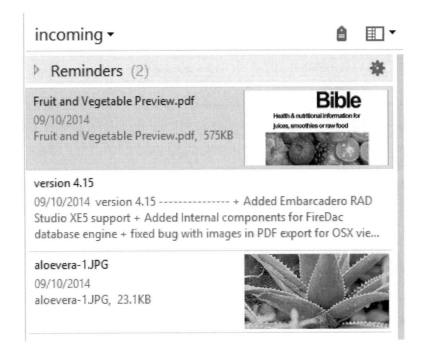

The first is a PDF file, which has been attached to a note and is fully readable from within Evernote:

Double click on the preview in Evernote to open the PDF file in your native PDF viewer.

The next document was a text file, and that text appears as the body of the note and is fully editable:

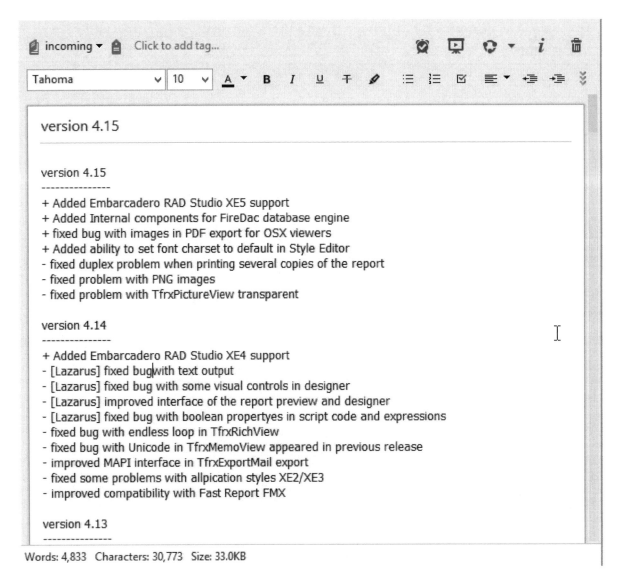

The final document was an image file. That's been added to a note, just like any other image would be if you attached one to a note:

One thing to bear in mind. Each document you save to your folder needs to be within the limits of file size offered by your Evernote account. That means 25MB for a free account and 100MB for a premium account.

Creating a Presentation from Notes

The presentation mode in Evernote is available on Mac, PC and iOS. It is not available currently on Android devices. However, the presentation mode is only available in Evernote Premium and Evernote Business.

Using the presentation mode, you can display your notes as a slideshow, much like you would in Powerpoint. You have an onscreen "laser pointer" and other options that you can explore by yourself.

PC

The first step in creating a presentation is to select the notes you want displayed in that presentation.

If all your notes are in the same notebook, select that notebook and choose your notes with SHIFT+Click or CTRL+Click.

If your notes are spread out in different notebooks, you can use the search features to find the notes and then select them.

E.g. let's say I want to create a presentation of my chocolate recipes.

I can search for chocolate recipes in any way we've looked at previously in the book. E.g. Select the recipe notebook and search it for the word chocolate. It returns 4 notes.

I can select all 4 notes by clicking the first one in the search results, holding the SHIFT key down and clicking the last one. I can select/deselect individual notes by CTRL+Click.

As you select the notes, you see a representation of them in Evernote as a collection:

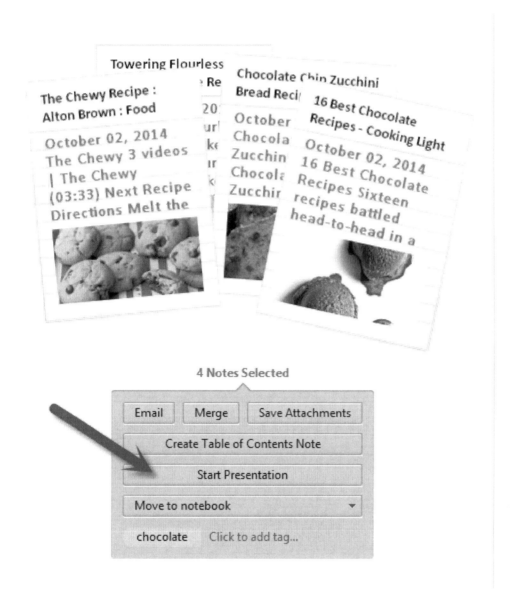

Click the **Start Presentation** button to begin.

Notice that from this screen, you can also move these notes to another notebook, or even **Create a Table of Contents Note**. This is a rather useful feature as it creates a note with links to the selected notes:

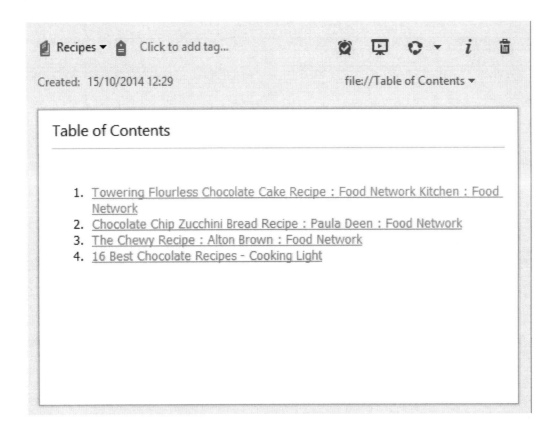

Mac

The first thing to do when creating a presentation is to select the notes you want included in the presentation.

If all notes are in the same notebook, select that notebook then choose your notes with Command+Click.

If your notes are spread out, you can use the various search features to find them. For example, let's say I want to create a presentation of my honey recipes. I could just open my recipes notebook and select the recipes, or, I could search for honey inside the recipe notebook with:

notebook:recipes honey

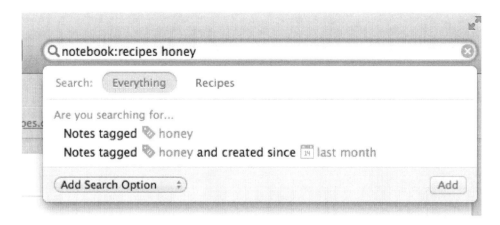

This will return a clean list of my three honey recipes.

I can then select them using Command+Click, or click the first item in the search results, hold the SHIFT key and click the last. This will select all of the recipes in the list, and is useful to remember if your list of notes is longer.

As I select the recipes, Evernote builds up a visual representation of my notes as a group:

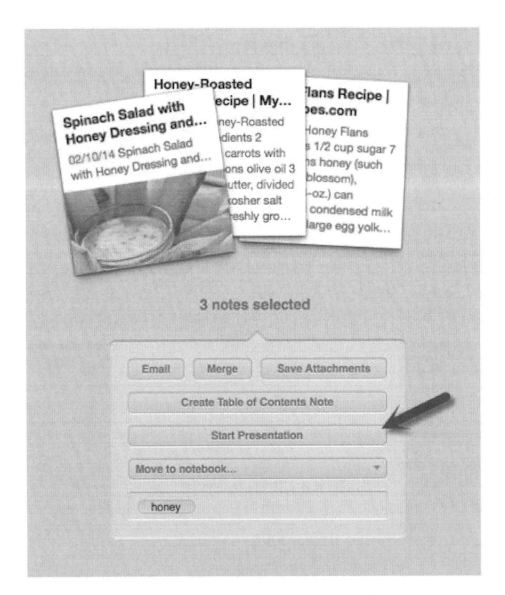

Once all are selected, click **Start Presentation** to begin.

Notice that you also have an interesting option here to **Create Table of Contents Note**. This is a useful option to have, and creates a note that links to all of the selected notes:

Recipes ▾   click to add tags

Created: 15 Oct 2014   Updated: 15 Oct 2014

Table of Contents

1. Honey Flans Recipe | MyRecipes.com
2. Honey-Roasted Carrots Recipe | MyRecipes.com
3. Spinach Salad with Honey Dressing and Honeyed Pecans Recipe | MyRecipes.com

iOS

To create a presentation on the iPad, you need to select the notes you want to include in the presentation.

By selecting, I don't mean tapping those you want. What I mean is that you need to have some kind of search results, only displaying the notes you want included.

It might be that you want to present all notes in a notebook, in which case this is easy. Simply select the notebook and all notes are then ready for the presentation.

If the notes are spread around different notebooks, I'd recommend you go in and tag those notes with something, maybe **presentation** (or copy them all to a presentation notebook you can then select).

You can then go back to the main sidebar, and tap tags.

Choose your **presentation** tag, and all notes tagged with that will be displayed.

Open the first note in the list by tapping on it.

Now tap on the menu button top right, and select **Present**:

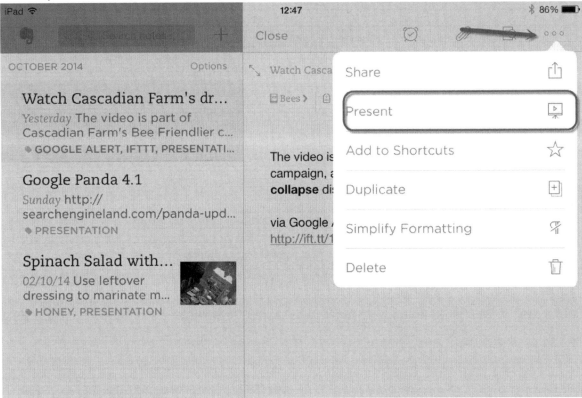

The slideshow will begin at the first note.

The presentation screen is scrollable, so if the note is long, just scroll down with your finger as you make your presentation.

Tapping the screen displays some buttons:

**Watch Cascadian Farm's dramatic
effort to save the bees**

The video is part of Cascadian Farm's **Bee** Friendlier campaign, aimed at educating
the public on **colony collapse** disorder and donating money to **bee** ...

via Google Alert - bee colony collapse **http://ift.tt/1vpjZcX**

Top left, you have a button to close the presentation.

Top right, you can toggle between day and night mode.

At the bottom, you can move between the "slides" with the up and down arrows.

GPS

If your mobile device has GPS, Evernote can take advantage of that and record the location that a note was created. That's pretty cool if you are on holiday, taking photos of your day trips. When you get back home, you'll be able to call up the exact location of every photograph.

Not only that, but if you use Android Evernote, you can use the GPS location attached to these notes to navigate back to that location (I haven't found a way of doing this on the iOS version).

Do you want to remember where you left your car next time you go out? Make sure GPS is turned on, and create an image note (using your phones camera) in Evernote. You'll then have the exact coordinates that you can display on a Google Map.

Android

If **Location** is running on your Android device, Evernote will try to store your location when it saves notes. This is the default behavior.

To prevent Evernote from using your location when saving notes, follow these instructions:

1. On your device, turn **Location** (GPS) ON. This needs to be on before you can turn it off in Evernote, otherwise the Evernote options are greyed out.
2. Open Evernote, and go to the **Settings** menu.
3. Scroll down the settings until you find **Note Creation**, and tap that.
4. Uncheck the top option **Use GPS Satellites** and also uncheck **Use wireless Networks**.

Now Evernote won't try to use location when saving notes.

To reinstate the use of GPS with notes, follow these instructions again, but check those boxes instead of unchecking them.

To find the location of a note, open the note and tap the Information button:

Audio recording

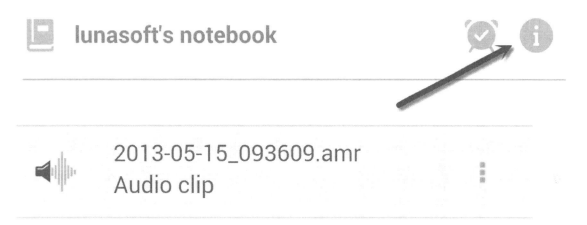

This opens up a small map to show you the location where the note was created:

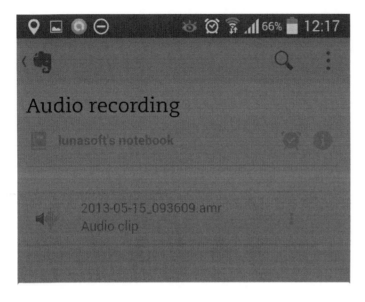

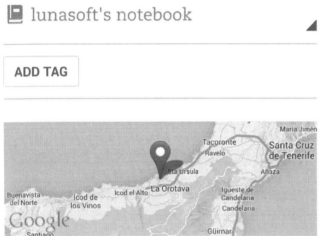

Updated: 15 May 2013 09:36:25

Created: 15 May 2013 09:36:25

Tap anywhere on the map and Evernote will open a full screen Google Map:

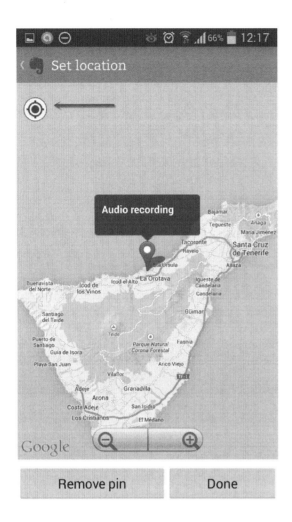

On this screen, click on the small location symbol top left, and your current location will be shown on the map. You can then see where you are in relation to where you were when the note was saved:

Your location will update as you move, so just move towards the pin and you'll be able to navigate towards the location where a note was saved. How cool is that?

iOS

To find the location where a note was created, open the note and tap on the Information button top right:

If your note has GPS data attached to it, you'll see something like this:

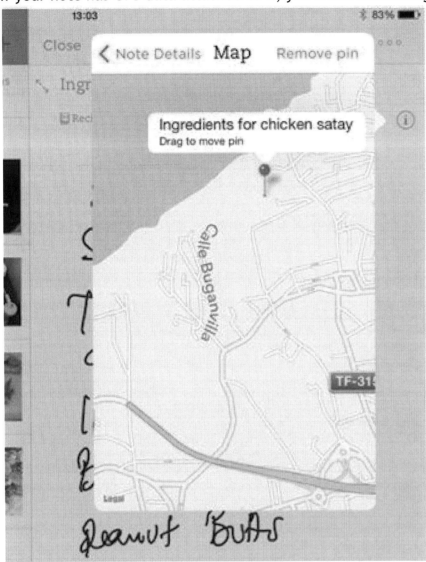

The pin marks the location where the note was created.

USES OF EVERNOTE

I'm sure your mind is buzzing with ideas on how you can use Evernote in your own life, but I've got a few suggestions as well.

1. **Keep a diary** – Since notes are time stamped and include location (if GPS is enabled), Evernote is a great place to keep a diary. It can be a diary of your life, a weight loss diary, or maybe a wine or beer tasting diary with your notes on the various drinks you tasted. If you are out touring the vineyards of France or Spain, you can have your GPS record locations with the notes, meaning you can always find your way back to a vineyard, no matter how many bottles you sampled.

2. **Keep holiday & travel notes**. If you are a traveler, Evernote can keep your travel logs, photos, notes, and the address of favorite restaurants (with a photo of the menu). If you find a nice secluded beach off the beaten track, with beautiful white sand and crystal clear water, photograph it. Evernote will add the location meaning you can always find it again, even years later.

3. **Scan important papers** that you might need when you are out an about.

4. **Scan receipts** for business or keeping your weekly budget.

5. **Scan your prescriptions**. This will help you keep a medical record of what you have taken and when.

6. **Record your kids growing up**. Take photos, voice messages, and hand-written or typed text notes. These notes have time stamps and location recorded (if you have GPS on your device), making everything so much easier to remember. If your kids draw pictures for you, photograph them and add them as notes. Again, the time stamp on these will help you remember how old your child was when they created that masterpiece.

7. **Project Notes** – keep a notebook for each major project you undertake, and add all thoughts, photos, and receipts as notes.

8. **Shopping lists**. Are you going out shopping for ingredients for a favorite recipe? If you are using Evernote Food, then you probably already have the recipe stored in Evernote. Alternatively, you could just create a notebook for your recipes, and have your favorites stored as notes. Whenever and wherever you are in the future, you can pull out your phone, and know exactly what you need to buy for that dinner party.

9. **Packing lists for travelling**. Do you always forget things when you go travelling? Your toothbrush or deodorant? Make a travel note listing everything you pack. While you are away, if there is anything you have forgotten, add it to the note, so next time you won't forget it. After your first trip, you should have a full and detailed travel list that you can refer to as you pack your bags in the future.

10. **Digital Scrapbook**. If you have a hobby, Evernote gives you a great way to keep a digital scrapbook. You can create notes on just about everything and use tools like WebClipper and Clearly to add important web documents to your scrapbook.

11. **Voice notes while on the move**. I often get ideas while I am out and about. Previously, I'd look around for a pen and paper. Now I pull out Evernote and record a short audio note to remind me when I get back home.

12. **Todo lists**. Is there something you want to do, or something you absolutely must do before a certain date? Creating a note with a reminder is a great way to keep on task. Create the note with a checkbox list of "todos", and set the reminder for the due date, or the day before if you think you'll need an extra day to get it organized.

13. **Photographs of things you need to remember occasionally**. License plates, printer cartridges, etc. I am asked occasionally for my car license plate (e.g. when checking into a hotel), and I actually don't know it, but Evernote does. I've got it stored in a note with a photo of my car. Similarly, I always forget the ink cartridge number I need for my printer. How quick and easy is it to take a snap of your old printer cartridge(s) and store it as a note?

Keyboard shortcuts

I'm not a big fan of keyboard shortcuts myself, other than a few Windows 8 specific ones, but I know a lot of people rely on their keyboard to get work done. Evernote has a lot of keyboard shortcuts, but rather than list them all here, you can find Windows keyboard shortcuts here:

https://evernote.com/contact/support/kb/#!/article/23168552

And Mac keyboard shortcuts here:

https://evernote.com/contact/support/kb/#/article/23168732

What Next?

We've covered a lot of ground, and I don't expect you to remember everything. The best way forward is to start using Evernote, every day. As you use it, you'll find new ways of simplifying and organizing your life.

Try some of my suggestions from the last section.

Come up with your own ideas on how best to use this tool.

Most of all just use it!

Contact Me

Firstly, thank you for buying my book. I hope you like it and find it valuable as you learn to use and incorporate Evernote into your life.

If you liked it, would you please leave a review on Amazon so others may benefit too? You can find the book by searching this identifying code: **B0OOMAXISK**

If you want to contact me for any reason, please do so via my website here:

http://andyjwilliams.co.uk

If you find great new ways to incorporate Evernote into your life, please let me know. I am always looking for innovative uses for Evernote!

If you have any comments about this book, or there are things you would like to see in this book, I'd be delighted to hear about them.

My other Kindle books

All of my books are available as Kindle books and paperbacks. You can view them all here:

http://amazon.com/author/drandrewwilliams

Made in the USA
Middletown, DE
13 December 2015